CO...

CHARACTERS

THE STORY OF SPIDER-MAN™

ORPHANED AT AN EARLY AGE, PETER PARKER LIVES IN QUEENS, NEW YORK WITH HIS BELOVED AUNT MAY AND UNCLE BEN. PETER LEADS THE LIFE OF A NORMAL STUDENT, WORKING AS A PHOTOGRAPHER AT THE *DAILY BUGLE* UNDER THE TUTELAGE OF PUBLISHER J. JONAH JAMESON, LONGING AFTER THE BEAUTIFUL MARY JANE WATSON AND HANGING OUT WITH BUDDY HARRY OSBORN.

ON A SCHOOL TRIP, DURING WHICH PETER AND HIS CLASSMATES ARE GIVEN A SCIENCE DEMONSTRATION ON SPIDERS, PETER IS BITTEN BY A GENETICALLY-ALTERED SPIDER. SOON AFTER, HE DISCOVERS THAT HE HAS UNUSUAL POWERS: HE IS ENDOWED WITH THE STRENGTH AND AGILITY OF A SPIDER AND THE ABILITY TO CLING TO ANY SURFACE, ALONG WITH A KEEN, ESP-LIKE "SPIDER SENSE." AFTER DISCOVERING THESE POWERS, PETER APPEARS IN A TELEVISED WRESTLING MATCH AND, ARMED WITH HIS NEW SPIDER STRENGTH, WINS THE MATCH IN RECORD TIME. HOWEVER, THE WRESTLING MATCH PROMOTER REFUSES TO AWARD PETER THE $3,000 PRIZE MONEY, ALLEGING THAT PETER WON TOO QUICKLY. SOON AFTERWARDS, PETER HAS THE OPPORTUNITY TO CATCH A BURGLAR FLEEING FROM THE PROMOTER'S OFFICE, BUT BECAUSE HE WANTS REVENGE, HE REFUSES TO STOP HIM. MOMENTS LATER, THE SAME BURGLAR KILLS HIS BELOVED UNCLE BEN.

AS SPIDER-MAN, PETER APPREHENDS THE BURGLAR BUT IS PLAGUED WITH GUILT FOR NOT BEING A HERO SOONER. DURING HIS TIME OF TURMOIL, PETER REMEMBERS SOMETHING UNCLE BEN ONCE TOLD HIM: "WITH GREAT POWER, COMES GREAT RESPONSIBILITY." PETER TAKES THIS TO HEART AND DECIDES TO USE HIS EXTRAORDINARY POWERS TO FIGHT CRIME.

MEANWHILE, MEGALOMANIACAL BUSINESSMAN NORMAN OSBORN, HARRY'S FATHER, IS UNDERGOING SOME CHANGES OF HIS OWN. AN EXPERIMENTAL FORMULA HAS BLOWN UP IN HIS FACE, INCREASING HIS INTELLIGENCE AND STRENGTH BUT ALSO DRIVING HIM INSANE. HE IS NOW THE GREEN GOBLIN, SPIDER-MAN'S ARCH ENEMY, WHO WILL PUT YOUNG PETER PARKER'S VOW TO FIGHT CRIME AND HELP INNOCENT PEOPLE TO THE ULTIMATE TEST.

SHOCKER

REAL NAME:	Herman Schultz
OCCUPATION:	Burglar/Now a Hired Assasin
SUPER POWERS:	[Only when wearing Battlesuit] Vibration Shield
ABILITIES:	Self-taught and Talented Engineer
WEAPONS:	Vibro-Shock units in Battlesuit
EQUIPMENT:	Battlesuit

THE SHOCKER™

HERMAN SCHULTZ WAS A CAREER CRIMINAL WHO DREAMT OF GETTING AHEAD —USUALLY AT THE EXPENSE OF OTHERS. HE CREATED A BATTLESUIT THAT WOULD FURTHER THIS AMBITION. WITH THE ABILITY TO VIBRATE THE AIR AROUND HIM, HE CAN CREATE DEVASTATING SHOCK WAVES.

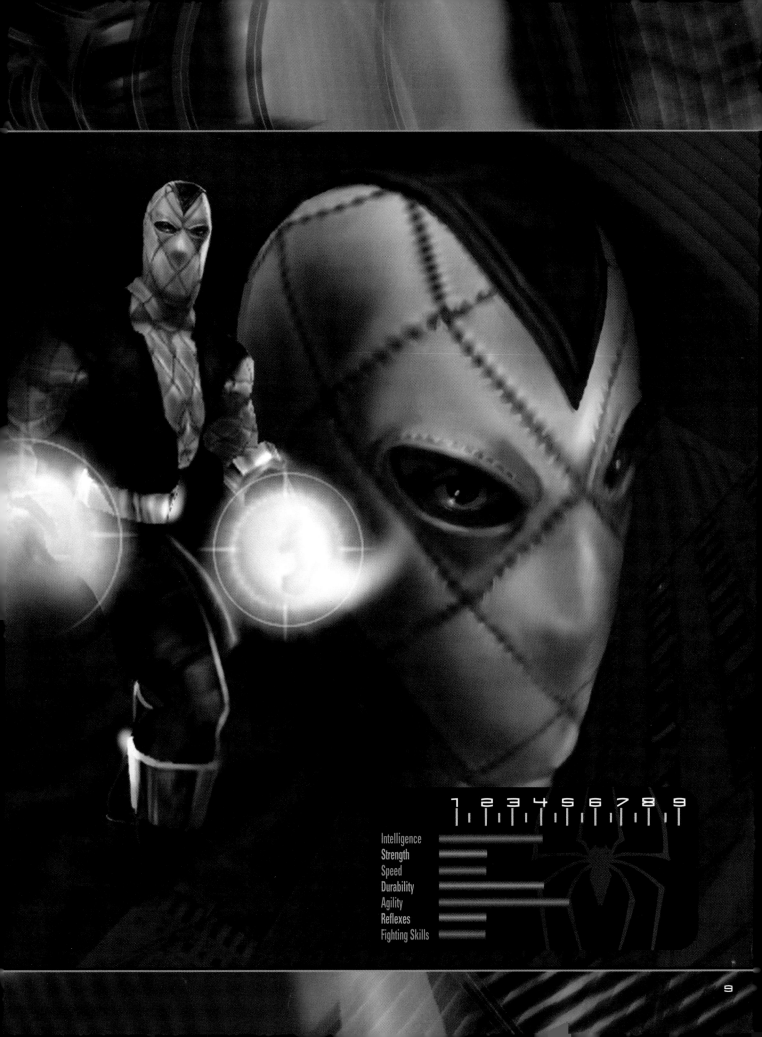

1 2 3 4 5 6 7 8 9 9

Intelligence
Strength
Speed
Durability
Agility
Reflexes
Fighting Skills

VULTURE ™

REAL NAME:	Adrian Toomes
OCCUPATION:	Professional Criminal Former Electronics Engineer and Business Owner
SUPER POWERS:	[Only when wearing Harness] Superhuman Strength, Vitality, and Athleticism
FLIGHT	Max Speed: 95 mph Max Altitude: 11,000 ft. Duration: Up to 6 hours
ABILITIES:	Electronics Engineer and Inventor
WEAPONS:	Plasma Pistol Various types of Grenades
EQUIPMENT:	Harness containing an Electromagnetic Anti-Graviton Generator

1 2 3 4 5 6 7 8 9

Intelligence
Strength
Speed
Durability
Agility
Reflexes
Fighting Skills

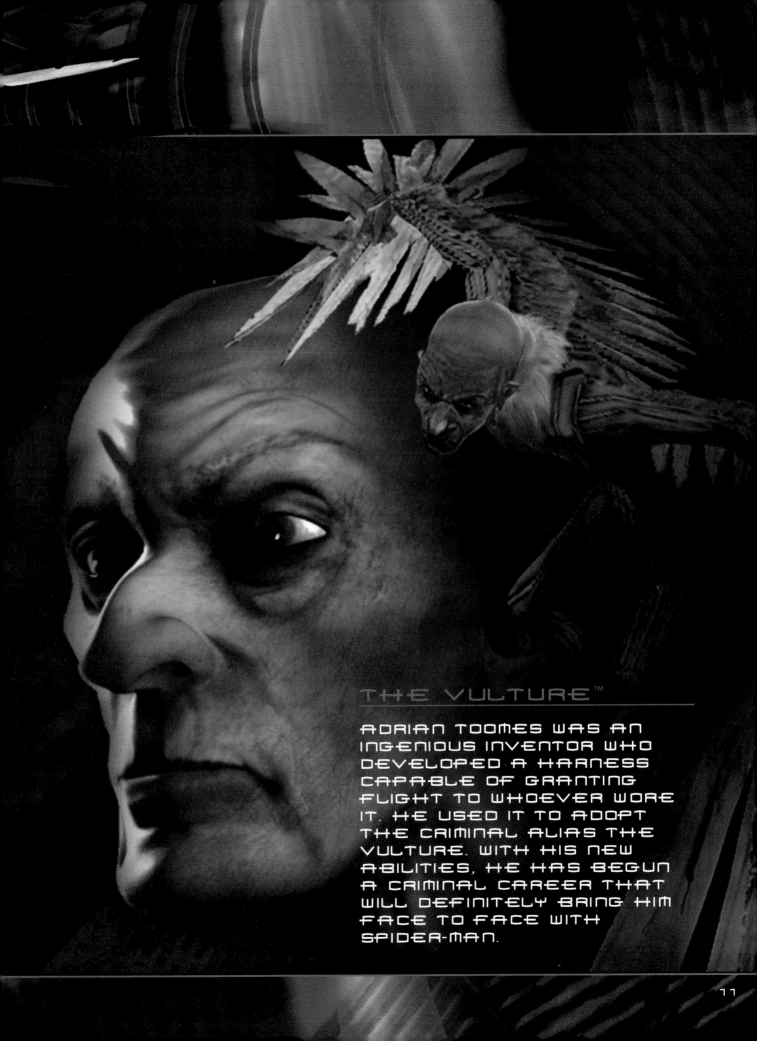

THE VULTURE™

ADRIAN TOOMES WAS AN INGENIOUS INVENTOR WHO DEVELOPED A HARNESS CAPABLE OF GRANTING FLIGHT TO WHOEVER WORE IT. HE USED IT TO ADOPT THE CRIMINAL ALIAS THE VULTURE. WITH HIS NEW ABILITIES, HE HAS BEGUN A CRIMINAL CAREER THAT WILL DEFINITELY BRING HIM FACE TO FACE WITH SPIDER-MAN.

SCORPION

REAL NAME:	MacDonald "Mac" Gargan
OCCUPATION:	Professional Criminal Former Private Investigator
SUPER POWERS:	Superhuman Strength, Agility, Speed and Stamina
WEAPONS:	Cybernetically-Controlled Tail and Pincer Grip
EQUIPMENT:	Battlesuit and Tail

THE SCORPION™

SHEATHED IN HIS BATTLESUIT, MAC GARGAN IS A MENACE TO THOSE WHO STAND IN HIS WAY. EVEN WITHOUT HIS BATTLESUIT, HE HAS SUPERHUMAN STRENGTH AND AGILITY. HOWEVER, HIS BATTLESUIT HAS A SCORPION'S TAIL THAT HE USES LIKE ANOTHER APPENDAGE—WITHOUT CONSCIOUS EFFORT. SCORPIONS ARE THE NATURAL PREDATOR OF SPIDERS AND THE SCORPION IS A DANGER TO SPIDER-MAN AS WELL.

1 2 3 4 5 6 7 8 9

Intelligence	
Strength	
Speed	
Durability	
Agility	
Reflexes	
Fighting Skills	

KRAVEN™ THE HUNTER

REAL NAME:	Sergei Kravinoff
OCCUPATION:	Big Game Hunter
SUPER POWERS:	Superhuman Strength, Speed, Agility and Stamina
ABILITIES:	Tracking, Hunting, and Trapping Skills
WEAPONS:	Darts, Spears, Nets, Axes, Traps, Whips, Poisons, Gases, etc.
EQUIPMENT:	Often Garbed in Animal Skins

KRAVEN THE HUNTER™

SERGEI KRAVINOV IS A MASTER OF THE HUNT. THANKS TO A MYSTERIOUS POTION, KRAVEN POSSESSES SUPERHUMAN STRENGTH AND SPEED, WHICH HE USES TO CAPTURE THE MOST ELUSIVE OF PREY. UPON REALIZING THAT THE WORLD'S MOST FEARSOME BEASTS WERE NO CHALLENGE, HE BEGAN TO HUNT A MORE FORMIDABLE SUBJECT—SPIDER-MAN.

1 2 3 4 5 6 7 8 9

Intelligence
Strength
Speed
Durability
Agility
Reflexes
Fighting Skills

GREEN GOBLIN™

REAL NAME:	Norman Osborn
OCCUPATION:	Scientist
SUPER POWERS:	Superhuman Strength Enhanced Intelligence Heightened Reflexes and Coordination
ABILITIES:	Talented chemist and engineer
WEAPONS:	Pumpkin Bombs Razor bats

THE GREEN GOBLIN™

NORMAN OSBORN IS A POWERFUL BUSINESSMAN AND WORLD-RENOWNED SCIENTIST. WHEN A LAB EXPERIMENT GOES TERRIBLY WRONG, OSBORN'S INTELLIGENCE AND STRENGTH ARE ENHANCED. BUT HE IS ALSO DRIVEN INSANE, AND NORMAN OSBORN ADOPTS THE GHOULISH PERSONA OF THE GREEN GOBLIN—SPIDER-MAN'S ARCH-ENEMY.

1 2 3 4 5 6 7 8 9

Intelligence
Strength
Speed
Durability
Agility
Reflexes
Fighting Skills

THE PARKERS

AUNT MAY AND UNCLE BEN ARE THE KIND RELATIVES WHO RAISE PETER IN THEIR QUEENS HOME AFTER HIS PARENTS ARE KILLED. AFTER UNCLE BEN'S TRAGIC DEATH, PETER VOWS TO DEDICATE HIS LIFE TO FIGHTING CRIME. IT IS BEN'S IMMORTAL WORDS, "WITH GREAT POWER COMES GREAT RESPONSIBILITY," THAT GUIDE PETER AS HE LIVES HIS DOUBLE LIFE AS SPIDER-MAN.

REAL NAMES:	Ben and May Parker
OCCUPATION:	May Parker is a home-maker

UNCLE BEN & AUNT MAY

MARY JANE

REAL NAME:	Mary Jane Watson
OCCUPATION:	Student

MARY JANE

MARY JANE WATSON, MJ TO HER FRIENDS, HAS BEEN PETER PARKER'S NEIGHBOR SINCE CHILDHOOD. UNBEKNOWNST TO HER, SHE IS ALSO THE GIRL HE'S BEEN IN LOVE WITH SINCE THE DAY HE SAW HER. AN ASPIRING ACTRESS, MARY JANE'S QUICK SMILE AND CAREFREE ATTITUDE HIDE HER SOMETIMES NOT SO PERFECT LIFE. EVEN THOUGH SHE IS DATING PETER'S ROOMMATE HARRY, PETER IS NEVER VERY FAR FROM MARY JANE'S THOUGHTS.

J. JONAH JAMESON ™

THE DAILY BUGLE

J. JONAH JAMESON IS THE EDITOR OF THE *DAILY BUGLE*, A TABLOID NEWSPAPER IN NEW YORK CITY AND PETER PARKER'S GRUFF, BUT KIND-HEARTED, BOSS. MUCH TO PETER'S DISMAY, JAMESON NEVER MISSES AN OPPORTUNITY TO USE THE NEWSPAPER TO QUESTION SPIDER-MAN'S MOTIVES, OFTEN PAINTING SPIDER-MAN AS A DANGEROUS VIGILANTE.

REAL NAME:	John Jonah Jameson
OCCUPATION:	Editor-in-Chief of the Daily Bugle
ABILITIES:	JJJ is a savvy businessman He can complain about anything for hours on end
EQUIPMENT:	Cigar Rolled-up Newspaper

BASIC WEB-SLINGING

MOVE	PS2	XBOX	GCN
Punch	■	X	B
Kick	●	B	X
Web	▲	Y	Y
Jump	X	A	A
Web Gloves	▲+Left	Y+Left	Y+Left
Web Dome	▲+Right	Y+Right	Y+Right
Impact Web	▲+Up	Y+Up	Y+Up
Web Yank	▲+Down	Y+Down	Y+Down
Web Swing	R2	R	R
Zip Line	R1	L Trigger	L Button
Look Around	R3	Right (press)	Z+Right
Camera Lock	L1 (hold)	White	Z (hold)
Re-center Camera	Right Analog ↓	Black	Z
Hang from web	▲+R1	Y+L Trigger	Y+Z Button
Ride enemy	X (hold)	A (hold)	A (hold)
Force Crawl	L3	Left Analog	N/A
Instant swing turn	N/A	N/A	N/A
Rotate Camera	Right Analog	C Stick	R Thumbstick
Directional Attack	Directional Buttons, Directional Pad, or + Control Pad + Punch/Kick (all platforms)		
Dodge	Directional Buttons, Directional Pad, or + Control Pad + Jump (all platforms)		
Zip Line Attack	Push Web Button while using zipline (all platforms)		
Twirl Yank	N/A		

MOVE	PS2	XBOX	GCN
Punch	■	X	B Button
Kick	●	B	X Button
Web	▲	Y	Y Button
Jump	X	A	A Button
Web Gloves	L2+■	L Trigger+X	L Button+B Button
Web Dome	L2+●	L Trigger+B	L Button+X Button
Impact Web	L2+▲	L Trigger+Y	L Button+Y Button
Web Yank	L2+X	L Trigger+A	L Button+A Button
Web Swing	R2	R	R Button
Web Zip	R1	White	L Button+R Button
Look Around	R3	Right (press)	Z Button+Right
Camera Lock	L2 (hold)	Black (hold)	Z Button (hold)
Re-center Camera	L1	Black	Z Button
Hang from web	L2+R1	L Trigger+White	L Button+Z Button
Ride enemy	X (hold)	A (hold)	A Button (hold)
Force Crawl	L3	Left Analog	N/A
Instant swing turn	L1+X	L Trigger+A	L Button +A Button
Rotate Camera	Right Analog	C Stick	R Thumbstick
Directional Attack	Directional Buttons, Directional Pad, + Control Pad + Punch/Kick (all platforms)		
Dodge	Directional Buttons, Directional Pad, + Control Pad + Jump (all platforms)		
Zip Line Attack	Push Web Button while using Web Zip (all platforms)		
Twirl Yank	Rotate stick while Web Yanking someone (all platforms)		

The classic control scheme is basically the same as the enhanced version, but you lose the ability to perform instant swing turns, and web moves are performed by tapping the Web button and then a direction on the pad, instead of a button. It is still possible to yank enemies around with Web Yank, but you have to quickly push another direction on the controller to do so.

BASIC WEB-SLINGING

Combine incredible agility, the ability to walk on walls, the strength to bend solid steel bars, and a reaction time faster than thought to create one of the world's most spectacular superheroes—Spider-Man. Of course, you might not possess his unique attributes, so to help you get used to using them, this section was designed to give you a firm grasp on the fundamentals of web-slinging.

SPIDER-MAN'S ARSENAL

Spider-Man has an impressive list of abilities, which can feel daunting at first glance. Mastering his moves is the first step to completing the game. Take advantage of the tutorial levels to get a feel for the controls. Focus particularly on web-swinging, wall-crawling, and controlling the camera.

Spider-Man's ground combat is something that will evolve as you play the game; there are many ways to use his moves, all equally effective. You can spend the whole game up close using various combos and his Web Gloves, or you can focus more on web tricks and staying back, using Web Yanks mixed with Impact Webbing and the occasional Web Dome to deal with the foes you encounter.

PUNCH

Spider-Man's fists pack considerable power; indeed, he is strong enough to lift a bus over his head. However, Peter is not going to use that power on a regular human, no matter what they've done. You can increase the damage by using Web Gloves though, and remember that Spider-Man's punches are faster than his kicks. While in the air, pressing the punch button near an enemy will launch Spider-Man at them.

KICK

Imagine a mighty Spider-boot to the face. Spider-Man's kicks inflict a bit more damage than his fists—at the cost of speed. They can't keep up with Advanced Web Gloves though, so you'll generally be using kicks on the ground only to start some combos. Use kicks after jumping into the air to lunge at a nearby enemy, or hold it while swinging to perform a Cannonball Kick.

WEB

Spider-Man's webbing can be used to tie up just about any enemy he encounters, putting them out of commission for a while. This is handy when dealing with packs, though it usually won't work on the various bosses that Spider-Man will encounter.

JUMP

Peter is quite nimble, and his jump is easily controllable while in the air. Quickly pressing the jump button twice will have Spider-Man perform a double jump, which is both very fast, and gives you a lot of height for evasion. It's also perfect for quickly leaping onto the ceiling.

WEB GLOVES

Wrapping his fists in layers of thick webbing, you can use the gloves to get a bit of extra power out of Spider-Man's fists. Performing the move twice will give you Advanced Web Gloves, which inflict even more damage. Remember that using any other type of webbing, swinging, or crawling will remove the gloves, so don't put them on unless you're ready to engage in serious combat.

WEB DOME

Surrounding his body in thick webbing, the dome serves two purposes: (1) it protects Spider-Man for a few seconds and (2) it blasts nearby enemies away from him. Using the dome twice in rapid succession will thicken the protection and deal more damage at the cost of a lot of web fluid. In general, you don't want to use this unless you're surrounded by enemies; even then, it may be better to dodge away. Still, if you have the web fluid, don't hesitate to use this tactic in an emergency.

IMPACT WEBBING

A concentrated ball of webbing makes for an excellent projectile, and you can charge it for a second to send Advanced Impact Webbing at your target. This is very useful in the air as well, automatically homing in on a locked target, no matter where Spider-Man is swinging.

WEB YANK

For putting an enemy temporarily out of the action, or for bringing a target closer so Spider-Man can deliver a personal beatdown, this move is what you want. You can also spin your target around, knocking down nearby enemies (and causing them terrible embarrassment).

WEB SWING

This is one of Spider-Man's most famous moves. The Web Swing lets you get around the city in style and, with a bit of practice, you can use it indoors as well. Remember that holding the button down will speed Spider-Man up, at the cost of some maneuverability (though you will get accustomed to this with time). When you are swinging at normal speed, if you are pressing away from a wall when Peter connects with it, he'll bounce right off, which is useful for swinging between narrow spaces.

ADVANCED IMPROVEMENTS

Throughout the game, you'll find Spiders that will augment your abilities. The Advanced versions of your Web Gloves, Web Dome, and Impact Web will make it easier to defeat those nefarious villains and their henchmen.

WEB ZIP

Spider-Man's Web Zip is very useful for getting him around. You can use it both while standing still or jumping to quickly reach the ceiling. And, while running, it's a great way to zip in the direction Spider-Man is facing. You can also press the web button while flying through the air. This will surround Spider-Man with webbing and damage any enemies he contacts. You can stop the zip by hitting jump at any time.

LOOK AROUND

This option is useful for two reasons. First, you can get a better feel for where Spider-Man is located, and second, you can use web attacks and the Web Zip with the aiming cursor. This is very handy for precision maneuvers.

CAMERA LOCK

The Camera Lock is absolutely critical for aerial engagements. and very useful on the ground as well. Locking the camera lets you focus your attentions on a single enemy. Even if you momentarily lose sight of your target, the Lock will make sure that your primary target remains the same.

RE-CENTER CAMERA

A seemingly minor control option, you'll find yourself pressing this quite often. Remember that while swinging in the air, if you do a simple reversal of direction, the camera will swing around naturally. However, there are many cases on the ground (particularly in tight spaces), where a quick tap will help you reorient yourself.

YO-YO

No one said Spider-Man couldn't play around, right? Spider-Man's classic hanging pose can be used to slide up and down from the ceiling. One of the more interesting functions is using a Web Zip from this hanging position. It will immediately send Spider-Man zooming off in a different direction. Use this if you need to get away from opponents quickly.

RIDING ENEMIES

This is one of the best combat options in the game. Granted, there are better ways to take out an enemy, but none look as cool as punching a villain in the head while riding on his shoulders. Holding the jump button while jumping on a foe's back lets Spider-Man cling, hold, and pummel the poor villain. Poor villain—right. It's also possible to steer the target slightly while he's confused and perform an impressive body slam by pressing the kick button. Hey, he was a wrestler for one match, remember?

FORCE CRAWL

This is useful in a few cases where you aren't certain of your jump, and you want to crawl to your target instead. Consider using the look around option in combination with the Web Zip for precise crawling.

INSTANT SWING TURNS

This is very useful in aerial chases. It allows Spider-Man to keep his momentum while swinging quickly. Press the jump button while web-swinging to have a chance to reorient yourself and head in a new direction.

ROTATE CAMERA

Good camera control comes a close second to good Spider-Man control. It's hard to use the web-slinger's abilities to their full potential if you're fighting with the camera instead of the villains.

DIRECTIONAL ATTACKS

Holding a direction on the Directional Buttons, Directional Pad or +Control Pad and pressing the punch or kick buttons unleashes an attack to either side of Spider-Man, or behind him. If you press forward, he'll perform a jumping attack that will knock down your target—be careful though, it's a bit slow. Use this when there's a group of enemies trying to get at Spider-Man. Target and hit the villain that is closest and continue to use this technique until you get a little breather.

DODGING

This is an extremely important move. A dodge lets Spider-Man roll, backflip, or dive out of danger. If he's ever getting pummeled, remember that dodges should have very high priority, and they'll let Spider-Man roll to safety.

COMBOS

Throughout the game, you'll find Golden Spiders that unlock more of Spider-Man's available combos. Each combo has a three button sequence to trigger it, and each one allows Spider-Man to perform a different acrobatic assault.

There are many combos (indeed, more than you will actually need), and they have two primary uses; first, they contribute to your Style ranking at the end of a level (repeatedly doing one combo is boring, right?), and second, many of them have an area knockdown, which is very useful when Spider-Man gets surrounded.

It is entirely possible to finish the game without a single extra combo, but they're fun to use, and cool to look at. Besides, you want that Style Bonus don't you?

COMBO LIST

COMBO	BUTTON SEQUENCE	FOUND IN LEVEL
Dual Fists	Punch, Punch, Punch	Starting Combo
Mule Kick	Kick, Kick, Kick	Starting Combo
Elbow Slam	Kick, Punch, Punch	Starting Combo
Field Goal	Punch, Punch, Kick	Search for Justice
Web Hit	Punch, Punch, Web	Search for Justice
Back-Flip Kick	Punch, Kick, Kick	Warehouse Hunt
Handspring	Kick, Jump, Kick	Birth of a Hero
Scissor Kick	Kick, Punch, Kick	The Subway Station
High Web Hit	Punch, Kick, Web	The Subway Station
Dive-Bomb	Punch, Jump, Jump	Chase Through the Sewer
Uppercut	Kick, Kick, Punch	Showdown with Shocker
Gravity Slam	Punch, Punch, Jump	Vulture's Lair
Dive Kick	Punch, Jump, Kick	Aerial Duel with Vulture
Sting	Punch, Kick, Punch	Aerial Duel with Vulture
Head Hammer	Punch, Jump, Punch	Corralled
Tackle	Kick, Jump, Jump	Scorpion's Rampage
Low Web Hit	Kick, Kick, Web	Coup d'Etat
Flip Mule	Kick, Kick, Jump	The Offer
High Stomp	Kick, Punch, Jump	Breaking and Entering
Palm	Punch, Kick, Jump	Chemical Chaos
Haymaker	Kick, Jump, Punch	Escape from Oscorp

ADVANCED MOVES	FOUND IN LEVEL
Advanced Web Gloves	Chase Through the Sewer
Advanced Web Dome	Birth of a Hero and Corralled
Advanced Impact Web	Escape from Oscorp

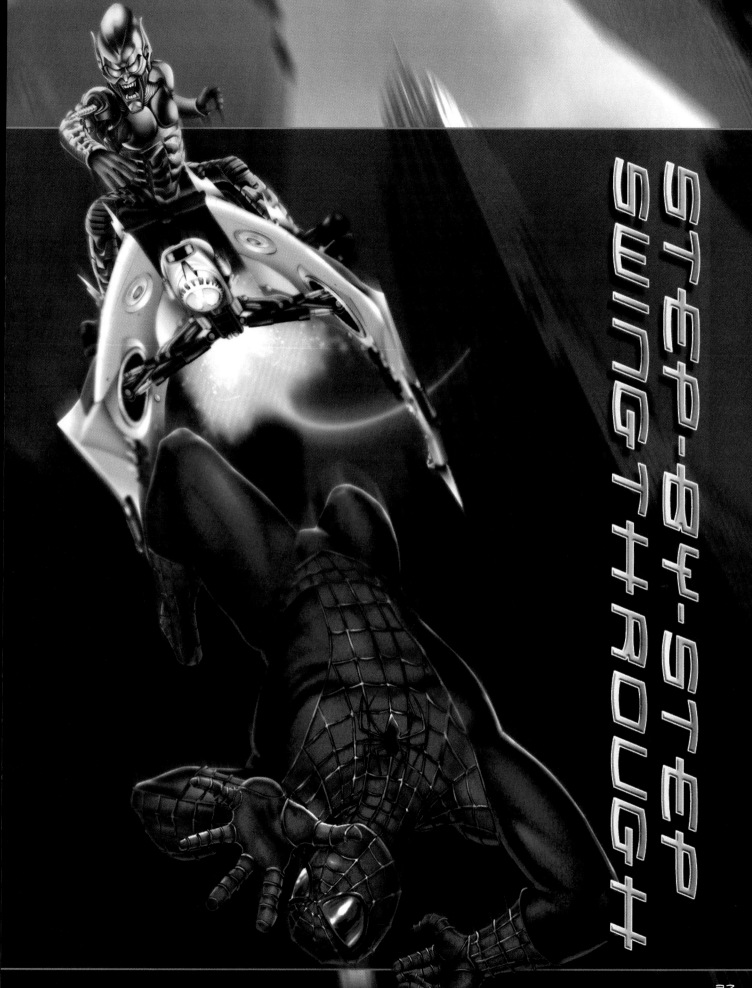

STEP-BY-STEP SWING THROUGH

SEARCH FOR JUSTICE

PRIMARY OBJECTIVES

- Find out who killed your Uncle
- Locate and apprehend the killer

BONUS OBJECTIVE

There's a Thug Bonus on this level. Defeat all of the thugs on this level to get the bonus. There are a few extra Skulls scattered around the level on other building tops.

GOLDEN SPIDER: YES   **SECRET AREA: YES**

STEP-BY-STEP SWINGTHROUGH

You begin your quest for revenge atop a statue on the edge of a skyscraper. The very first **Golden Spider** of the game is directly below you. Drop off the edge and then crawl back up the wall to retrieve it. This gives Spider-Man the Field Goal combo.

GOLDEN SPIDER

FIELD GOAL . . . . .PUNCH PUNCH KICK

Now you get a bit of practice using the Spider Compass. Use the directional indicator and Spider-Man's Web Swing to reach your next objective: a showdown with a few Skull thugs. Watch the elevation indicator beside the compass as well. Spider-Man is indicated by the red bar, the objective is in blue. Your first target is close. Swing over until the Spider Compass turns white and land on the rooftop.

ON THE RIGHT TRACK

You'll know you're on the right track when you can see an Activision building in the distance.

The second **Golden Spider** of the level can be found at the top of another building. Just head straight from your starting point and turn to the right until you see a beige and black sky-scraper with vertical stripes. On top of the building, there are a few extra walls that construct a hall of sorts. Look around the rooftop to discover the Web Hit combo.

GOLDEN SPIDER

WEB HIT . . . . .PUNCH PUNCH WEB

When you land on the building, you get your first chance to exercise Spider-Man's newfound strength on a few goons. Basically, any combination of attacks will defeat the gang members, so use the opportunity to practice web-slinging. Hit them with Impact Webs or pull them within range using the Web Yank.

TEST YOUR NEW COMBO

Try out your new combo on one (or both) of these thugs. The final hit knocks your target back a good distance. This can be handy in some situations, but several of Spider-Man's later combos will eclipse this one for general utility.

Next stop, another rooftop. Your goal is a bit higher and farther this time, so use the opportunity to practice swinging around the city. Remember, while Peter may be angry right now, you don't have a time limit to contend with. Once you're done sightseeing, follow the Compass and land on top of the building it leads you too.

Another pair of thugs needs to be knocked out before you can move on. They wander around a bit and may be difficult to spot at first. If you have trouble finding them, jump off the building, get a little height swinging, and look down. You could also use the Camera Lock to keep your sights focused while you drop from the air. Once you find them, deliver the beatdown. Once these Skulls are taken care of, the next waypoint activates.

You guessed it, yet another rooftop awaits. This is the second to last though, so start swinging. Try "fast swinging" by holding the Web Swing button down. Spider-Man will pick up speed and race across an area. This is handy in big outdoor areas and critical in some of the later levels when someone doesn't particularly want to be caught. Those pesky villains!

TAKE A TOUR AROUND TOWN

Do some sightseeing while you're practicing Spider-Man's aerial acrobatics. There are a couple of interesting buildings located here, you'll probably recognize at least a few of the names.

Two more goons wait at the next location, but this time, one has a gun. Spider-Man isn't going to take much damage from him even if you ignore him completely while dealing with the other thug. However, keep in mind that this is just a taste of things to come. Try restraining him with webbing, or use the Web Yank on him. By the time the gunman recovers from getting tossed around, you should have dealt with his buddy. When both of the thugs are finished, take off for your final destination.

PETER'S FIRST COSTUME

Spider-Man's costume on this level (and the next few) is the original. When Peter came across an opportunity to accept a wrestling challenge for some extra money, he put a mask on and got in the ring with Bone Saw McGraw.

Simply put, Peter didn't even realize that he was going to be "Spider-Man" at the time. He simply wanted to earn some quick cash and needed a quick way to disguise his identity—and his powers.

Upon discovering that his Uncle Ben's murder could have been prevented if only he had acted, Peter had a change of heart, and soon after, a change of costume as well. Taking his uncle's words, "With great power comes great responsibility" to heart, Peter realized that the innocent needed a guardian—Spider-Man was born.

WARNING

Beware of enemies using guns. Spider-Man isn't bullet proof; after all, he's no Superman. He can take a surprising amount of damage in a short time around packs of enemies using long range weaponry. If Spider-Man ever gets badly hurt, back off—swing away, jump away, or roll away. There's usually health in a safer area on the level, wherever you happen to be.

Web Swing off the building and follow the Spider Compass. You'll wind up near where you began the level and this tower top has what you've been seeking. One of the gang members here knows where Uncle Ben's killer is located; he just needs a bit of encouragement to offer the information.

Dispatch the Skulls here to trigger a cut-scene. The Skull helpfully directs you to a warehouse at the edge of town. The thugs here aren't any more difficult than what you've faced earlier on the level, but if you get surrounded, use your Web Dome and stun them all.

FIRE AWAY!

At this point, there's no need to save web fluid, you're almost done. So, take the thugs down with whatever web-tactics you feel most comfortable with.

WARNING

There's another gun-wielding thug here, consider taking him out first.

On a rooftop a short distance to the left of Spider-Man's starting location (and a bit to the left of the final thugs, if you've been following the compass) is a building with a pair of thugs on it. If you check there, you can find a woman's missing purse. Consider it an early good deed on Parker's part.

Spider-Man's done here and you've found out all that you can. Follow the Compass to reach the top of the warehouse, ending the level.

LEVEL DIFFICULTY

WAREHOUSE HUNT

PRIMARY OBJECTIVE

● Find Uncle Ben's killer

BONUS OBJECTIVE

There's a Stealth Bonus on this level. Avoid being seen by the enemies instead of fighting them.

GOLDEN SPIDER: YES   **SECRET AREA: YES**

STEP-BY-STEP SWINGTHROUGH

Being your first indoor level, this will give you some practice in enemy avoidance, close quarters fighting, and (the fun part) throwing large objects around. As you enter the warehouse through an open door, Spider-Man will wind up in a small room on the second floor. Take a moment to look around. Interact with some of the objects in the room by pushing the punch or kick buttons while standing next to them.

NEW TOYS

Spider-Man can pick up almost anything in the various indoor levels. (Heck, he can even pick up civilians in a few cases.) To pick up an object, get next to it and press the punch button. Then, press the bunch button again to throw it at your target.

Be especially careful when dealing with explosive objects; they will detonate on impact. If you throw them at an enemy directly in front of our favorite web-slinger, he'll take significant damage.

NEW TOYS PART 2

If your surrounded and don't have the time to do that, try pressing the kick button while next to an item. Spider-Man will just grab the object and toss it in the direction that he's facing. (Try this on a stack of tires!)

If you're in Camera Lock mode, the object will be sent at whoever (or whatever) you are locked on to.

Once you're done housecleaning, go through the door and down the steps into the small garage. Pick up the **Golden Spider** in the stairwell to unlock the Back-Flip Kick, an acrobatic and damaging combo. The exit you need to reach is another small door on the opposite side, and there are two approaches you can use to reach it. Directly—beatdown the thugs using all the objects in the room, or quietly—sneak across the ceiling and drop down. There is a **Health Spider** located on the upper catwalk if you happen to need it.

BACK-FLIP KICK . . . .PUNCH KICK KICK

In this next room, a pack of Skulls will immediately try to jump Spider-Man. Once again, use the terrain to your advantage—throw it at them! Defeating the first group will cause a second mob to attack. Once they're down, this area is clear. Head to the back and exit through the garage door.

SECRET AREA

There is a stack of crates midway through this room, crawl up to the top left and you'll go through a small gap to reach the Secret Area. There is a Health Spider here, but nothing else of interest.

Your entrance does not go unnoticed this time. This large room has a great, big semitrailer on one side, and the man you're hunting is standing near it. When the Skulls realize Spider-Man has arrived, the killer runs through a garage door just in front of the semi. Unfortunately, the door's closed and jammed behind him by another member of the Skulls in a control room up above. You need to get up to that control room and replace the Fuse to open the door.

REPLACE THE FUSE

Remember, once you recover the Fuse and replace it, you need to return to this room and go through the garage door the killer exited through to finish the level.

You could fight the thugs here, but they're heavily armed and you may want to simply avoid them. Head around the semitrailer, but be careful. As soon as Spider-Man goes around the corner, a Skull in a forklift will rush him. Peter's Spider Sense goes nuts, and you should double jump or Web Zip to the ceiling immediately to avoid being crushed.

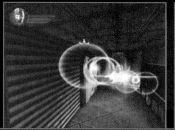

WARNING

Be careful! The forklift will kill Peter instantly, forcing you to restart the level. Don't go around the semi unprepared.

SPIDER SENSE IS TINGLING

Spider-Man's Spider Sense is used throughout the game to indicate a variety of different threats. In this case, it's a forklift; in later levels, it will be anything from a blast of energy from the Shocker to an approaching security guard.

EXTRA HEALTH

If you do decide to fight the thugs, there are two Health Spiders in the area. One is on top of some crates in the center of the main room; the other is in a small side area near the forklift's previous parking spot.

Head to the area where the forklift rushed Spider-Man and check around for a ventilation shaft cover. Use your Web Zip to go straight up and into the tunnel, then crawl along until you reach a branch. The path straight ahead is blocked by a surging arc of electricity and you'll have to turn aside. Crawl along the shaft and drop out of the shaft to reach a small room; you'll notice that there's a switch in it. Trip the switch to cut off the electricity blocking your path, then return to the shaft and crawl through the newly-opened route.

WHERE AM I?

If you get disoriented in the vent shaft after disabling the electricity, look on the bottom of the shaft. There are burn marks and scoring on the metal where the arc was; that's the path you need to follow.

When you drop out of the shaft past the electrical barrier, you'll be in the control room with the fuse box (but no Fuse). Remember this room (and the vent shaft cover on the ground); you'll need to come back here when you get the Fuse.

Leave through the door at the back and enter a small room with a pair of Skulls waiting for you. Knock them out, then leave through the room's only other exit to face another pair of Skulls. Once they're down, check the door—the guy with the Fuse is behind it and it's locked.

ANOTHER VENT SHAFT

There's a vent shaft on the floor of the small room—you'll need to go up it in a minute.

You can't get in there for now, so check the hall for some **Web Fluid** and look to the left of the door. There's an open passage. Jump up and head through it to discover another small room with a switch. Flip the switch, return to the small room where you fought the first pair of thugs, then Web Zip up where the vent shaft cover is.

Travel through the shaft and drop down at the end to reach the unfortunate Skull with the Fuse. He'll take a bit more of a beating than his cronies, but a bit of superhuman muscle will convince him to hand it over. Once you've got the **Fuse**, head back to the control room and use it on the control panel to activate the garage door in front of the semi.

CLOSE QUARTERS COMBAT

When you're fighting in extremely close quarters, don't try to web up enemies—particularly when you're facing a pack. Once you've acquired combos that can knock down groups of enemies, that's what you'll want to use. Don't hesitate to use your Web Dome if you get completely surrounded. Remember that dodging and rolling will get you out of traps as well.

You're all done here—head up the vent from the control room, drop back down to the large area with the semi, and head through the door in front of it. Uncle Ben's killer is almost in your grasp. Vengeance is almost yours.

You need to defeat two groups of thugs to reach the exit from this room. Use all the objects in the area to your advantage by flinging them at the Skulls; once they're defeated, this level is finished.

LEVEL DIFFICULTY

1
2
3
4
5

BIRTH OF A HERO

PRIMARY OBJECTIVE

- Defeat Uncle Ben's Killer

BONUS OBJECTIVE

You need to finish the level quickly to get this Time Bonus.

GOLDEN SPIDER: YES   **SECRET AREA: YES**

STEP-BY-STEP SWINGTHROUGH

The goal of your revenge-driven search is near. The small room you have entered from the last level has a vent cover on the ceiling—you know what that means. Web Zip up into the vent and crawl through. Drop into a large storage area filled with crates—and a lot of hostile Skulls. Use the stacks of boxes for cover and look around for piles of tires and explosive projectiles to use. There is a **Health Spider** tucked away behind one of the crates if you need it.

CHOICES

There are a couple of exits from the vent shaft, but it doesn't matter which one you take. They all lead to the same enemy-infested room.

WARNING

One of the Skulls is armed with a sub-machine gun. Be careful. If you want to take him out quickly, run away to get some breathing room, then put on your Web Gloves and attack. The extra damage you inflict will easily be enough to drop him quickly.

Once you're finished with the goons, leave through the only available exit. You'll enter a narrow hall filled with hot steam. A quick tutorial on the Look Around Cam will ensue, and when it's finished, Web Zip to the end of the hall. A short walk around a corner will reveal the **Golden Spider** on this level, this one giving Spider-Man the highly useful Handspring.

GOLDEN SPIDER

HANDSPRING . . . . . . .KICK JUMP KICK

You can pick up the Advanced Web Dome here in the room just prior to the steam hallway, but you have to reach the room undetected. To do so, crawl through the vents carefully before you reach the thugs, and use the ceiling to avoid notice.

GOLDEN SPIDER

ADVANCED WEB DOME

HANDSPRING COMBO

The Handspring is one of Spider-Man's best combos. It will launch him backwards, then spring back with a kick that will knock ALL nearby enemies down. This is perfect for dealing with large groups of enemies; you can keep just about anything perpetually stunned.

The next room holds a giant pack of Skulls (most of the gang it would seem), and one of them is holding a key that's required for you to progress. Zip up to the ceiling before you get completely surrounded and scout out the room. There are **Health** and **Web Fluid Spiders** on the ceiling and a tutorial tip and a **Health Spider** on the catwalk as well. When you're ready to deal with the gang, play hit and run. Drop down, throw a few handy objects, and then dart away. If you do get surrounded, use your Web Dome to repel the mob.

EXPLOSIVE RESULTS

The explosive objects are Spider-Man's best means of dealing with large groups. The Web Dome is too expensive in terms of the amount of Web Fluid used. While the Handspring will knock enemies down, explosives tend to keep them down.

Once the thugs are defeated, take the key and head through the small door located in a corner of the room. Pick up the **Health Spider** right past the door if you need it and then head down the hall. Web Zip straight up to the ceiling to skip the stairwell. Your encounter with the killer is a room away. Walk down the hall and go through the door to find him.

SPIDER-SENSE

Think of this as an early warning device.

This ability allows Spider-Man to sense danger of all types. His spider-sense manifests itself as a tingling in the back of his skull. The intensity changes based on the proximity and potential of the danger. If it's not immediate, it will register as a minor tingle; if the danger's close, it will build into sensory-blinding blast. It's even active while he sleeps!

Don't be fooled into thinking that his spider-sense only works for villains. It is also effective in pointing out mishaps, pranks, icy sidewalks, etc. Basically, you can't sneak up on Peter trying to slap a "Kick Me" sign on his back.

In addition to warning Spider-Man of danger, his spider-sense can also trigger his superhuman reflexes before the threat even occurs. Often, Spider-Man is already dodging the attack before it is even thrown. Obviously, this frustrates his opponents to no end.

Our favorite web-slinger also uses his spider-sense to track villains. He simply uses it like a geiger counter, heading toward the direction that causes the most tingling. Peter's developed special Spider-Tracers that he can follow with his spider-sense to facilitate this.

Lastly, his combination of spider-sense and superhuman agility and reflexes becomes most effective in the middle of a fight. Have you ever wondered how he has the time to think up all of his witty insults and repartee to distract his opponents? Well, he can react without consciously thinking about it—it's all instinct.

BOSS FIGHT

UNCLE BEN'S KILLER

Get up on the ceiling immediately. This Skull is armed with a sawed off shotgun that inflicts grievous damage on Spider-Man at close range. There are regenerating **Health** and **Web Fluid Spiders** in the corners of the ceiling, so be sure to take advantage of them.

This thug will wander around below in the maze of crates and boxes. Take advantage of this situation and observe safely from your perch on the ceiling. You may want to hide among the rafters and then leap down onto him. Make sure to put on some Web Gloves before attacking.

When you're ready to attack, drop down near him, then either jump or roll out of the way of his initial shot. Before he has a chance to follow up, pummel him with a combo, then head back up to the ceiling.

WARNING After you've damaged him a bit, the thug will sometimes drop a flashbang. If he does, get Spider-Man out of the way—jump back onto the ceiling. The blindness makes fighting impossible.

Repeat this pattern a few times and your hunt for revenge will be complete, as will Spider-Man's realization of his powers and the responsibility they entail. This ends the origin series of levels and you begin the main story next level.

OSCORP'S GAMBIT ™

PRIMARY OBJECTIVES

- Get some pictures for Jonah

BONUS OBJECTIVE

Defeat the Hunter Killer drones

GOLDEN SPIDER: NO

SECRET AREA: NO

STEP-BY-STEP SWINGTHROUGH

The origins section of levels is complete. In this level, Spider-Man appears as he is now, with his famous costume, and an assignment from Jonah to get a few pictures. No problem, all you need to do is pull off a few tricks in the air.

SPIDER-MAN ™

Peter Parker, after being bitten by a genetically altered spider, becomes Spider-Man, a hero of superhuman strength with the ability to cling to any surface. Spider-Man, inspired by his late Uncle Ben's immortal words, "With great power there must also come great responsibility," dedicates himself to fighting crime, while living a double life as a superhero and working student.

For the first trick, start swinging. Don't worry about making it fancy; just launch off the building you're standing on and head forward. Now you need to pull off the first move. Jump while you're swinging, then press the Web Swing button again to start swinging in another direction.

QUICK CHANGE

This technique will serve you well throughout the game. There are three steps to the process.
1. Press the jump button while you're webswinging.
2. Face in the new direction in which you'd like Spider-Man to go.
3. Press the Web Swing button once again to continue on the new path.

This is good advice, keep it in mind any time you need to quickly change directions. Getting comfortable with it will let you whip the camera around effortlessly, which is handy when dealing with aerial enemies.

Next up, Spider-Man's in for a bit of practice with the Camera Lock mechanic while in mid-air. Swing near the target and lock the camera onto it. That's simple enough. Once that's been snapped, shoot an Impact Web at the target. It doesn't matter where you are; even if the indicator is red, the webbing will be on target. Once you destroy the target, you're done here.

TARGET LOCK

Target locking is critical in mid air engagements. You don't always need to use it on the ground, but in the air, it helps greatly when you are trying to keep track of a target in a large area.

Well, you thought this was done. While heading back with the shots, Peter gets accosted by some unfriendly, green, floating, and deadly Hunter Killer robots. These drones are a bit of a pain and you need to wipe them out to finish off this level.

To destroy them, keep the camera locked, and punch them when you get close (if the indicator is green, or if you are just above your target, there's a good chance you'll hit). Alternatively, you can jump and then kick, which will have the same effect. Whichever you do, hit the Web Swing button as soon as you hit your target, swing away, then come back for another pass.

EXTRAS

There are Health and Web Fluid Spiders on buildings in the area, but be wary of enemy attacks while you stop to pick them up. You shouldn't need either if you dispatch the Hunter Killer drones quickly.

If you're a dexterous button pusher, you can slam the same enemy several times in rapid succession, quickly destroying it. If you wish, using your Impact Web to good effect here is also an option. Once thirteen of the drones have been defeated, you're done, and Spider-Man is safe.

NORMAN OSBORN

Norman Osborn is a powerful businessman and world-renowned scientist. When a lab experiment goes terribly wrong, Osborn's intelligence and strength are enhanced. But he is also driven insane, and Norman Osborn adopts the ghoulish persona of the Green Goblin, Spider-Man's arch-enemy.

ONE MORE SHOT

Here's something to keep in mind. Spider-Man's automatic Web Fluid regeneration will quickly give you just enough to fire off a single Impact Web. This is very useful in this type of engagement. Mix in physical attacks and, by the time you've come around for another pass, you'll have enough Web Fluid to fire another Impact Web.

THE SUBWAY STATION

LEVEL DIFFICULTY: 1 2 3 4 5

PRIMARY OBJECTIVE

● Protect the Civilians from the Shocker and his thugs

BONUS OBJECTIVE

Finish off the robbers attacking the civilians and guards quickly to get this Time Bonus.

GOLDEN SPIDER: YES   **SECRET AREA: NO**

STEP-BY-STEP SWINGTHROUGH

An armed robbery downtown means some innocent civilians need Spider-Man's assistance. Spider-Man arrives in time to stop the Shocker's getaway—you'll have to catch up with the Vulture later. When you go after the Shocker, he takes hostages and attacks the security guards in the subway station. When you begin the level, a guard directly in front of Spider-Man is being attacked. Beat off the pack of thugs to save him.

GOLDEN SPIDER

When there are only a few thugs left, don't knock them out—check the back of the subway terminal on the side to find the Golden Spider, this one granting the Scissor Kick.

GOLDEN SPIDER

SCISSOR KICK . . . . .KICK PUNCH KICK

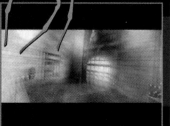 

NEW COMBO

The Scissor Kick is hard-hitting, but does little to knock away other nearby enemies. Don't hesitate to use these thugs for a bit of sparring practice to get a feel for it.

After defeating the goons attacking the security guard, Spider-Man's Spider Sense goes off—a civilian and a security guard are in trouble. Follow your Spider Compass up the stairs and into the small room where a single thug blocks your entrance.

Knock him out of the way, run into the back room, and rescue the civilian. Then help out the security guard. Using your Web Yank on a few of the thugs works well; it's faster than tying them up with webbing and gives you time to protect your charges.

HIGH WEB HIT . . . . .PUNCH KICK WEB

High Web Hit is nearby, located on the ceiling above the steps leading down to the main floor area. Grab this when you get a break from some of the thugs (or when there are no civilians in immediate danger).

Once the civilian and the guard are safe, leave the room and return to the main terminal. You'll spot another guard in trouble directly across from your position, but he's only being attacked by two thugs. Swing over and help him out.

The Shocker will return and, in an effort to buy himself time to escape, he blasts one of the support columns directly above a civilian. You've got to save the distracted guy on the cell phone before the pillar falls on his oblivious head. Swing over to him, pick him up (using the punch button), and run over to the giant Spider Pad on the ground. Drop him off by pressing punch again.

Rescuing the civilian will attract the attention of another trio of thugs. Once they're out of the way, Peter's Spider Sense will go off again. Two guards are in danger; this pair is a bit deeper in the terminal. Get to them and beat off their attackers.

ZIP LINE ATTACK

When you're dealing with large crowds like this and (for whatever reason) you don't have the Handspring combo, use a Zip Line Attack to knock out a bunch of enemies. Just hit your Web Zip button while heading towards a group, then press the webbing button while in the air. The whole pack will get knocked down, giving you more time to deal with them.

THE SHOCKER™

The Shocker's one of the more dangerous foes that Spider-Man has come across. Although he was initially a small-time criminal, he decided to create a special battle suit that sent shock waves from his wrist gauntlets. He used these to open safes quickly so that he could make a quick, and clean, getaway. Since then, he's been working as a hired assassin as well.

Spider-Man realizes the threat that he faces each time he meets the Shocker, and no longer considers him to be a small-time criminal. Although he remains focused on increasing his wealth through theft and extortion, he has begun to increase the level of his targets. Lately, he's been targeting armored cars as a quicker way to gain the riches he so craves.

CHASE THROUGH THE SEWER

LEVEL DIFFICULTY: 1 2 3 4 5

PRIMARY OBJECTIVE

● Catch the Shocker

BONUS OBJECTIVES

Complete the level quickly to earn this Time Bonus.

Knock out all of the thugs to obtain the Thug Bonus. This is pretty easy, since they're all located along the path you must take. Don't miss any in the valve area.

GOLDEN SPIDER: YES   SECRET AREA: YES

STEP-BY-STEP SWINGTHROUGH

Once the guards are safe, you're free to chase the Shocker into the sewers. Of course, the Shocker has left an unfriendly welcoming party behind just for Spider-Man; there are a lot of thugs between you and a showdown with the Shocker. Indeed, a pair of his underlings comes rushing down the hall at you as you start the level. Treat them to a spider-style beatdown and move on down the hallway.

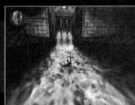

You'll enter a small caged-in room with a thug here—and he's got a key you'll need to beat out of him. Smack him around a bit with your combo of choice, then retrieve the key when it drops.

Go through the door with the glowing switch—the key will open it automatically when you approach. Beyond is a sewer channel with some fast flowing water (and unlike so many other heroes, Spider-Man won't drown if you dunk him). One way is blocked, so head up the channel the opposite direction. Mind the thug with the sub machine gun though… He's guarding a **Health Spider** if you need it when you're done dealing with him.

Take the passage on the side of the channel across from the Health Spider. Once there, knock out the pair of goons that attack and then follow the hall to a large, open sewer drain. There will be a catwalk across it. There's a **Web Fluid Spider** in the center; pick it up if you need it. Drop down.

THE SHOCKER'S™ SUIT

Wouldn't everyone want a battlesuit like the Shocker's? Using his engineering expertise, the Shocker built his battlesuit in an effort to help him break into safes more quickly. He didn't pull his punches when he did so.

For his first suit, the Shocker developed two Vibro-Shock units that are fitted on his wrists and hands. By causing vibrations through the air, the Shocker was able to create high-pressure air blasts with devastating effects.

Since its inception, the Shocker has adapted and expanded the vibro-shock units to cover his entire battlesuit, not just his hands. With this, he can create a shield of sorts using the same theory. By vibrating the air around him, he can withstand impacts that would normally take him out. The shield also allows him to get out of almost anyone's grasp; it's difficult to hold onto something that is consistently striking its captor with shocking forces.

Recognizing the force of his suit and the potentially lethal powers that it contained, the Shocker used a thick foam-lined fabric to absorb the impact caused by the Vibro-Shock units. With this battlesuit at his disposal, the Shocker easily climbed out of the ranks of the small time and into the big leagues.

There's a thug waiting for you when you land. Above you, another pair of robbers waits on the ledge that wraps around the circular pit. Two switches are on the sides of the ledge; you need to trigger them. Once the switches are depressed, the sealed door at the bottom will open; head through it.

WARNING
Be careful here, Spider-Man will be the focus of a lot of gunfire. There's a Health Spider on the ledge if you need it. Remember, a quick knockdown or Web Yank will put a gunman out of commission quickly.

There's another sewer channel past the door; crawl and Web Zip up the wall or ceiling to get through quickly. Upon reaching the exit, the Shocker will make a getaway through a large sewer pipe. He gets Vic, one of his flunkies, to turn on the water in the pipe once he runs. Then, the Shocker steals the valve and runs off. You need to retrieve the valve in order to continue the pursuit.

Enter the room, knock out the thugs, and then swing over to the top of the pipe to find the **Golden Spider**. Once you've learned the new combo, follow Vic and retrieve the valve.

GOLDEN SPIDER

DIVEBOMB . . . . . . .PUNCH JUMP JUMP

WARNING
Be careful when you go for the Golden Spider! The water below is electrified; a single slip could cost you.

Vic is in this tiny maze of grating and side passages along with a bunch of the other thieves. He'll try to run away, but you can lock him in place with some webbing. Give him a few knocks to the head when you get the chance. He takes quite a beating, but he'll eventually drop the valve you need. Take it back to the previous room to use it.

EXTRA SPIDERS

There's a Health Spider in the middle of this room and a Web Fluid Spider in one of the small side passages.

NEW COMBO

The Divebomb you earn here causes Spider-Man to smack his opponent, then launch himself in the air and come crashing down. It's impressive, but not so useful near edges. Oh, it also knocks enemies down, and it does so quicker than the Handspring…

Use the valve to stop the flow of water from the pipe, then swing on in and proceed down until it opens above you. Hop out and give a pugilistic greeting to the pair of thugs waiting for you. If you look on one of the walls, you'll spot a ladder. Head up to the room above and then press the switch on the wall—this opens the secret area in the room you just left.

 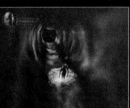

GOLDEN SPIDER

ADVANCED WEB GLOVES

SECRET AREA

Once the switch in the pipe room is activated, head back down the pipe and drop to the bottom of the room you came from. You'll find the entrance to the Secret Area.

When you return to the formerly electrified water, after hitting the switch, you'll find the highly useful Advanced Web Gloves tucked away within this room. If you're playing in Enhanced Control mode, you may find the Advanced Impact Web.

You're getting there. Once finished with the secret area, continue down the waterlogged passage. You'll be confronted by a trio of thugs, but they're nothing that our web-head can't handle. Besides, it provides something to practice the new Divebomb on. Knock them out and head down the passage until you reach another water channel.

Go down the channel and, when you enter the large room beyond it, the channel gate will slam shut behind Spider-Man. It's not difficult to guess what happens next—a set of thugs attacks. There's more Divebomb practice for Spider-Man it seems; when you defeat them, another group will enter and attack. If you need a breather, head for the upper area and grab the **Health** and **Web Fluid Spiders**.

When all of the thugs are finally knocked out, two things must be done to exit. Drop down to the very bottom of the room and enter one of the two side rooms. Once you've pressed the switch and obtained a key from one of the thugs, swing up to the top of the room. Leave through the newly accessible door. The Shocker waits just ahead.

SHOWDOWN WITH THE SHOCKER™

PRIMARY OBJECTIVE

- Defeat the Shocker

BONUS OBJECTIVE

You'll have to hustle to get this Time Bonus. In addition, staying at a distance in the fight with the Shocker won't be an option.

GOLDEN SPIDER: YES   SECRET AREA: YES

STEP-BY-STEP SWINGTHROUGH

There are two parts to this level. First, you need to get close enough to the Shocker to do any damage (while he sends a barrage of blasts at you). Next, when you do catch up to him, you need to put him down. You start the level just behind the Shocker, but he's up ahead at the end of the Subway, launching blasts of energy at you.

Head up the subway tunnels—*carefully*. The Shocker will send a blast down the tunnel as soon as you poke your head out. Get to the gaps in the sides of the tunnels on your approach to remain safe from harm.

WARNING Spider-Man can take a few hits—very few. You're better off just being cautious and making your way up the tunnel slowly and carefully.

Once you manage to get up close, the Shocker will run away and block your path by destroying the passage behind him. You can't clear it, but there is a way around it. Pull the pair of levers, one on either side of the blocked passage. The subway car on the left will move out of the way revealing a new route, one which will take you directly to the Shocker.

Be ready when you take the new path. There's a sewer channel past the top of the stairs; the **Golden Spider** will start to float away as soon as you enter the area. Quickly chase after it swinging or using the Web Zip if it gets away. Once you retrieve it, head down the tunnel to your duel with the Shocker.

GOLDEN SPIDER

UPPERCUT . . . . .KICK KICK PUNCH

SECRET AREA

Picking up the Golden Spider here counts for the Secret Area bonus at the end of the level.

BOSS FIGHT

THE SHOCKER™

The Shocker is an impressive adversary; he has power in spades. He does not, however, have any extreme agility, which gives you the only advantage you need. Play keep away with him, staying at long range and dodging his blasts.

Any time his guard is down, send a ball of Impact Webbing at him, and dodge any counter-attacks. There is plenty of Health and Web Fluid in the corners and top of the room if you need it.

CONTINUED

The Shocker will occasionally change positions in the room. He'll head from the upper area to the lower area and back, depending on Spider-Man's location. It doesn't matter much where is, as long as you have the Camera Lock mode on. With this enabled, just send webbing flying at him—it'll be accurate.

UPPERCUT

The Uppercut combo inflicts impressive damage and is best used against single, strong targets. The lack of an area knockdown means it is bad against groups and really bad against groups with guns.

The Shocker will occasionally use a tornado attack, pulling Spider-Man into close range. You can resist this by running in the opposite direction, or by swinging away.

His last powerful attack is a short range shockwave that will hit Spider-Man if you're anywhere near him. That's another reason to stay at a distance and pelt him with Impact Webs.

SHOCKER DAMAGE

If you're gutsy enough to get close to him with some Advanced Web Gloves on, you can inflict some heavy damage with either a Scissor Kick or the Uppercut Combo you just acquired.

Hitting him with enough webbing from a distance will take him down. That's one super-villain off the wanted list. Don't get comfortable, the Vulture is still out there and you've got to catch him.

LEVEL DIFFICULTY 1 2 3 4 5

VULTURE'S™ LAIR

PRIMARY OBJECTIVE

● Climb the Vulture's Tower

BONUS OBJECTIVE

There's a Time Bonus on this level, so speed through it. This is pretty easy to do, given that speed is your friend on this level.

GOLDEN SPIDER: YES

SECRET AREA: NO

STEP-BY-STEP SWINGTHROUGH

With the Shocker safely captured, Spider-Man can turn his attention to the Vulture. Luckily for him, the Vulture flew away when the heist went off and he got away. Now, our favorite webhead's on the case and after that big old bird. He's waiting for Spider-Man at his tower and he's prepared an unpleasant welcome for him. All you need to do to finish this level is climb—that is, climb and dodge all the explosives. To begin, go through the short hallway past where you begin the level and start climbing the stairs.

Vulture will taunt Spider-Man as he climbs (repeatedly) and toss explosives down the stairs. Double jumping over them makes avoiding these explosives more of an annoyance than a real threat.

Always keep moving upwards. Use your Web Zip and lots of double jumps to speed your ascent. The middle of the tower is occasionally open, and you can find **Health Spiders** within.

THE VULTURE'S TOWER OF PERIL

The Vulture's roost has a simple layout. There's a single staircase spiraling up around the center section of the tower and most of the dangers are on the stairs. Use the middle section to avoid any nasty threats that the Vulture may have in store for you.

Watch out for the proximity bombs and mechanical spiders as well. The proximity bombs aren't too dangerous—just get past them quickly. The spiders however, will pursue you doggedly, and detonate when they get close. There's a slight delay on the detonation though; a quick double jump will get you out of the way safely.

EXPLOSIVE EVASION

It is very possible to quickly cruise through this level. Move fast, jump often, and use your Web Zip when possible. If you do get trapped by an explosion or two, remember that Spider-Man's rolls will allow him to dodge most dangers, working even while he's getting pounded on (unlike his jumps).

Upon reaching the halfway point, the Vulture will set off a large explosion that destroys part of the tower above you starting a fire. A giant log begins swinging through the middle of the tower. The trick to dodging it is to get below it on the edge of the stairs and, when it swings from you, Web Zip straight past it.

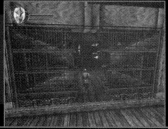

After you've cleared the log, you'll enter a slightly maze-like section of the tower. Parts of the path will be barred, but the stairs and the center of the tower are broken in places. That seems like the perfect way to get through.

PATH-FINDING

When your path gets blocked for the first time, backtrack for a second and check the center. There's a break in the wall, go inside, and climb up through the hole in the opposite side. Any time you get stuck, look around for a hole in the middle.

Don't miss the **Golden Spider** here. You need to drop through a section of broken stair and walk around the tower to find it.

THE VULTURE™

Like most of the super-villains that Spider-Man encounters, the Vulture is driven by his greed and lust for power. Adrian Toomes used his abilities as an engineer and inventor to create a body harness that would allow a person to fly. He finished the design and became the Vulture.

The Vulture and Spider-Man have become heated adversaries. With a predator like the Vulture on the loose, Spider-Man better turn his spider-sense on to its highest setting!

GOLDEN SPIDER

GRAVITY SLAM . . PUNCH PUNCH JUMP

Occasionally, the Vulture will blow out a section of the floor, opening up a path through this area. Continue upwards until you're out of the mini-maze.

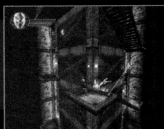

The final run is ahead of you. The explosions will come thick and heavy, so keep moving and jumping. If the floor gets blasted out from under you, quickly Web Zip back up and continue. When you get to the top of the tower, the Vulture will attempt to make a getaway and Spider-Man will go swinging after him.

WARNING

If you get stuck to a wall while you're jumping up, get off quickly. The spiders will home in on you, explode, and knock you down into more explosions.

VULTURE™ ESCAPES

PRIMARY OBJECTIVES

- Catch the Vulture
- Protect Civilians from the Vulture's rampage

BONUS OBJECTIVES

Once again, there's a Time Bonus for getting through the level quickly. Quickly web up the structures Vulture attempts to destroy and resume the pursuit.

The second bonus objective is to maintain a Close Proximity to the Vulture. Stay close to him at all times. Fast swinging is the only way to do this.

GOLDEN SPIDER: YES   SECRET AREA: YES

STEP-BY-STEP SWINGTHROUGH

Your first experience with an aerial chase begins here. You need to keep up with the Vulture at all times. The meter at the top of the screen will gauge your distance from him and, if falls too far behind, it's game over. Hold the Web Swing button to gain speed while you're chasing him. Switch directions by jumping and swinging again quickly and use regular swings when you need to maneuver around buildings.

GUIDE ME!

The Vulture leaves a long green contrail behind him while he flies; this visual aid will let you keep up with him even you lose sight of him around a building. Take advantage of it, and stay close.

WEB-SLINGING TIPS

The first part of the chase takes you between very narrow gaps in the buildings. Remember that if you're swinging normally, you won't stick to a wall while you're pressing away from it. Spider-Man will just bounce off.

A short distance into the chase, the Vulture will detonate the supports of a billboard, high above a busy street below. Quickly land, activate Camera Lock to target the struts, and cover them with web fluid. You don't need to feel overly rushed while you're doing this. If you've been following the Vulture closely, you'll have enough time to do your job and get back to the chase.

THE VULTURE'S™ HARNESS

Who among you hasn't dreamt of gaining the power of flight? Well, Adrian Toomes fulfilled his dream by creating an electromagnetic harness granting him that very same ability.

The harness contains an anti-graviton generator that allows him to conquer the skies. Flapping the bird-like wings attached to the undersides of his arms, the Vulture can attain speeds of up to 95 miles per hour. Not only that, but the maximum known altitude that he's gained reaches 11,000 feet. (That's just over two miles!)

One of the beneficial side-effects of wearing the harness is that it also increases his strength, vitality, and athletic ability to superhuman levels. These traits allow him to resist the mighty winds above the earth's surface and endure the cold and the physical beating that a normal human would receive at those heights.

Having had years to perfect his method of flight, the Vulture has grown accustomed to wearing his harness and hates to be out of it. The powers granted to him by this harness have fooled him into thinking that he can't live without them.

WARNING

This might seem strange, but if you're very adept with your web swinging, it's possible to go *too* fast. There are a few points where you'll be right on top of the Vulture, and you may want to back off slightly. He'll be able to hit you more easily and you can lose sight of him if he makes a sudden direction change.

A long pursuit comes next. The Vulture will lob even more nasty projectiles at you, but they're avoidable. Remember that you can jump to evade them. Staying above the Vulture will help (1) keep him in sight and (2) give you time to dodge his attacks.

EXTRA SPIDERS

There are Health and Web Fluid Spiders on a few of the building tops. If you swing just right, you can pick them up and keep moving. Don't waste too much time going for them though; if you take a lot of damage, just restart the level—it's very short.

SPIDER-MAN'S™ SUPERHUMAN POWERS IN DETAIL

Superhuman Strength

Spider-Man possesses incredible strength and stamina. Having the ability to lift a car over your head is a wonderful feeling (try it in the game). Some of the damage that Spider-Man endures would crush a normal person; however, he shrugs the blows off and gets back into the fight.

Superhuman Speed & Agility

Sure, superhuman strength is a remarkable power, but it's his amazing speed and agility that make Spider-Man so recognizable. His acrobatic maneuvers make him extremely difficult to hit. While he's bouncing around the villain, he can rain down blows while being an amazingly elusive target.

Superhuman Reflexes

When combined with his speed and agility, Spider-Man's reflexes become an unmatchable power. His reflexes are many times that of a normal human. Using this ability, he can attack an opponent from multiple directions and befuddle them. The typical thug that Spider-Man runs into doesn't stand a chance. Using walls, ceilings, cars, or anything in reach, Spider-Man can leap from one object to the other and land blows as he springs by. The villains don't stand a chance!

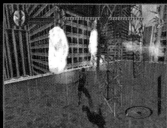

The Vulture will tire of the chase and try to get you off his tail feathers by endangering civilians once again. He'll blast the supports of a water tower. Just as you did before, quickly land, web up all of the damaged struts, and resume the chase once again.

At this point, the Vulture starts to pull out all the stops and begins throwing even more debris at Spider-Man, but he's losing steam. Keep up the pursuit and the level will end shortly.

AIR DUEL WITH VULTURE™

LEVEL DIFFICULTY: 1 2 3 4 5

PRIMARY OBJECTIVE

● Defeat the Vulture

BONUS OBJECTIVE

The Time Bonus on this level isn't too difficult to beat. Deliver a quick beat down to the Vulture to achieve this bonus.

GOLDEN SPIDER: YES   **SECRET AREA: NO**

STEP-BY-STEP SWINGTHROUGH

BOSS FIGHT

THE VULTURE™

Take a break from beating on the bird-man to investigate the huge building. If you can get all the way to the top, you'll be well rewarded with the Sting **Golden Spider**, and if you check the sides, you can find Dive Kick as well. Make sure you knock Vulture down before you go crawling around though, you don't need him hounding you.

GOLDEN SPIDER

DIVE KICK . . . . .PUNCH JUMP KICK

GOLDEN SPIDER

STING . . . .PUNCH KICK PUNCH

Another first for Spider-Man, this time you must fight a mid-air duel against the Vulture. You begin the level locked onto him; you should remain that way for the duration of the fight. The only time you'll want to break contact with the Vulture is if you need to grab some health or a **Web Fluid Spider** from the sides of the building.

AERIAL COMBAT

If you have difficulty in this fight, replay it a few times. Many of the upcoming levels take place in the air, so this level will provide some much-needed practice on inflicting damage against a moving target.

CONTINUED

When the level begins, get close to the Vulture and press the punch button; or, get close, jump, and press kick. Either method results in punishment being inflicted against the Vulture.

ALTERNATE ATTACK

To land on the Vulture's head, hold the jump button while falling towards him. This is quite useful for delivering some extra damage. This isn't easy to do, however, as it lacks the auto-targeting of Spider-Man's other aerial attacks.

You can also stay back (while in the air) and launch Impact Webs at the Vulture. As long as you're reasonably close, he won't have time to pull any evasive maneuvers.

After inflicting enough damage against the Vulture, he lands on a nearby building. This also affords you a great opportunity to inflict some real damage. As soon as the Vulture heads for the building, swing down to the ledge, put on some Web Gloves, and unleash a combo.

After the Vulture takes a few hits, he returns to the air. You must now repeat the cycle to damage him again. Get back in the air, knock him back down, and then combo him repeatedly on the building.

The Vulture isn't too tough, as long as you watch your health and Web Fluid. You can outlast him even if you're having a difficult time landing hits.

LEVEL DIFFICULTY

CORRALLED

PRIMARY OBJECTIVES

- Protect the Scorpion
- Destroy the Spider Slayers

BONUS OBJECTIVE

Keep the Scorpion healthy to get the Health Bonus. This is easy to do if you keep the Spider Slayers near him knocked down.

GOLDEN SPIDER: YES   SECRET AREA: YES

STEP-BY-STEP SWINGTHROUGH

This mission might have you scratching your head, as you must protect the Scorpion at all times. Remember though, this is early in Spider-Man's career and he doesn't any history with Scorpion—yet. You'll start the level locked on to a nearby Spider Slayer; most of the pack will be attacking the Scorpion. Quickly get in and start mixing it up.

If you didn't get it on the thid level (Birth of a Hero), there's an Advanced Web Dome on the ramps between the second and third floors. Don't leave the Scorpion alone for too long if you try to get it. Pick this **Golden Spider** up when the Scorpion moves to the upper floor after the Spider Slayers' numbers have depleted.

GOLDEN SPIDER

ADVANCED WEB DOME

THE SCORPION™

Having been given his powers for the sole reason of destroying Spider-Man, the Scorpion has become one of Spider-Man's most fearsome foes. In nature, scorpions hunt and prey upon spiders. That theory has carried through into the life of Spider-Man.

The Scorpion is stronger than Spider-Man and has much quicker reflexes as well. The Scorpion continues his life of crime and finds himself facing off against our web-slinger when their paths cross. Believe it when you hear that these battles are legendary.

Because there are a lot of Spider Slayers, you'll want to use attacks that knock down groups of enemies. Use whichever combo you're most comfortable with to accomplish this.

WARNING

The Spider Slayers have two nasty attacks. They'll paralyze you and they'll burn you. The paralysis in combination with the flames is a very dangerous duo, as the damage inflicted is extreme. Be careful and keep them knocked down.

The Scorpion will move around the garage a bit, fighting any nearby Spider Slayers. However, you don't want him doing it alone. Don't get tied up fighting the mechanical arachnids while the Scorpion takes a beating. He is the focus of this level after all.

TIME TO RECOVER

There are Health Spiders scattered around the parking garage, so don't hesitate to disengage from the melee and go searching around a bit if you get badly wounded. The Scorpion can deal with the Spider Slayers while you recharge.

Spider-Man can throw the cars in the garage—to impressive effect. If you're locked onto a Spider Slayer, toss a car directly at the metal bug and watch the fireworks.

THE SCORPION'S™ BATTLESUIT

The Scorpion's costume is actually a battlesuit. It was developed to be used in combination with the superpowers that Mac Gargan attained when being subjected to a series of treatments.

The battlesuit itself contains some enhancements that make the Scorpion a truly deadly adversary. It was constructed with two layers of steel mesh separated by a single layer of insulated rubber. This allows the Scorpion to shrug off any small arms fire that may target him. It also serves to protect him from the various effects of his tail.

The tail is a true marvel and is cybernetically linked to the Scorpion's brain stem. To him, the tail is simply another appendage to be used in defeating Spider-Man. The tail can be whipped at speeds surpassing 90 miles per hour and measures seven feet in length. It's covered by the same material as his suit and is equally impervious to most types of damage.

The tail has been modified to emit acid and force blasts. It's got a sharp blade-like pinion attached to it as well. The tail itself can be used as an extra appendage or as a spring, propelling the Scorpion up to 30 feet in the air. The combination of the Scorpion's powers and his battlesuit is sure to wreak havoc in Spider-Man's future.

GET OVER HERE!

If you're targeting a Spider Slayer that gets on the wall, just use a Web Yank to pull it down. The best part is getting a free hit in while it's on the way.

All you need to do to finish the level is destroy all the Spider Slayers. Mop them up to trigger a conversation with the Scorpion—and the end of the level.

SCORPION'S™ REVENGE

PRIMARY OBJECTIVES

- Defeat the Scorpion

BONUS OBJECTIVE

No Pickups Used. Don't get any of the pickups on the level (except the Golden Spider). This is doable, though challenging. Keep the Scorpion knocked down with the right combos to pull it off.

GOLDEN SPIDER: YES

SECRET AREA: NO

STEP-BY-STEP SWINGTHROUGH

BOSS FIGHT

THE SCORPION™

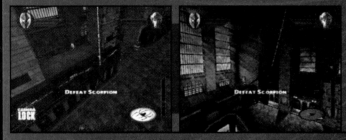

The conversation with the Scorpion turns ugly, as he's convinced that Spider-Man is out to get him. Soon after, you're fighting him in the subway terminal you visited much earlier during your fight with the Shocker.

This is **not** an easy fight. The Scorpion inflicts tremendous damage in a very short amount of time, and even a single slip up can cost you the fight. Staying at a distance and using Impact Webs won't work either, as he avoids them.

Before you get too involved in the fight, check the tops of the pillars, the **Golden Spider** is found atop the column that the Shocker blasted.

GOLDEN SPIDER

TACKLE . . . . .KICK JUMP JUMP

TACKLE COMBO

The Tackle combo is useful against the Scorpion. It's similar in appearance to the Handspring, and fast enough to knock him flat on his back.

When you're ready to engage the Scorpion, jump or roll to get in close, get off a combo, and quickly retreat before he can retaliate. Consider getting close and baiting him into attacking first to open him up for a counter-attack, but you must be fast to pull this off safely.

If the Scorpion heads for the walls, use a Web Yank to get him back on the ground where you can damage him. If you see a really nasty attack coming, use a Web Dome to protect yourself.

Unsurprisingly, the Scorpion's tail is a dangerous weapon. It fires lasers at Spider-Man, and also acts as a nasty bludgeoning tool. Scorpion will also grab and crush Spider-Man if you aren't careful.

Fall back and grab the **Health Spider** if you need it. The Scorpion's laser fire can be avoided if you're quick with your jumping and swinging. After inflict enough damage, the Scorpion finally drops. Spider-Man is beginning to realize Oscorp is up to no good, and a confrontation with the Green Goblin is approaching.

COUP D'ETAT

PRIMARY OBJECTIVES

- Save Mary Jane
- Chase the Green Goblin

BONUS OBJECTIVE

There's a Time Bonus on this level.

You need to deal damage to the Goblin quickly, and web up the damage he does to the city fast to get this bonus.

GOLDEN SPIDER: no

SECRET AREA: no

STEP-BY-STEP SWINGTHROUGH

The Green Goblin makes his appearance with a bang, and in the process puts Mary Jane in danger. Swing down to the panda and pick up Mary Jane, then swing over to the nearby building rooftop and place her on the glowing spider symbol.

MARY JANE

Mary Jane Watson, MJ to her friends, has been Peter Parker's neighbor since childhood. Unbeknownst to her, she is also the girl that he's been in love with since the day he saw her. An aspiring actress, Mary Jane's quick smile and carefree attitude hide her sometimes not so perfect life. Even though she is dating Peter's roommate Harry, Peter is never very far from Mary Jane's thoughts.

Now you have your hands full. You must deliver some punishment to the Green Goblin to get him to run. Your fighting experience against the Vulture will serve you well in this encounter. Lock the camera onto the Green Goblin and then swoop in to inflict some damage.

After causing substantial damage to the Green Goblin, he turns and runs—don't let him get away! After you both veer around a few buildings, he sends some Pumpkin Bombs at a radio tower.

You need to land and repair the support beams before the tower falls. Use some webbing to fix the structure; keep in mind you have a time limit. It's best to avoid using camera lock on the supports; just face each one and shoot webbing until it solidifies.

After fixing the tower, the Goblin takes off once again. Get into the air and cause some damage to him to make him run, then chase him as he flees.

This chase is longer than the previous one, but you can make it easier by staying high up in the sky. By taking the high route, you can avoid his attacks and the camera lock still tracks him. This enables you to follow him even when he goes behind buildings.

SPIDER-MAN'S™ WALL-CRAWLING

One of Spider-Man's most versatile, and unnerving, qualities is his power to adhere to any surface he desires. He needs no rope, or in his case a web, to climb the side of a building or up a wall. Spider-Man can simply cling and climb.

Although it's unknown exactly how this power works, it's function has been observed on many occasions. Regardless of how smooth or slippery a surface may be, Spider-Man can cling to it if he concentrates enough. He's been seen scaling skyscrapers, bridges, ceilings, almost anything he can reach. In fact, that's how Spider-Man can swing through a city on his webs. He simply clings to the web while it's in his hand, releases it, and focuses on the new line when he shoots it. There's no danger of losing his grip— almost.

If Spider-Man is knocked unconscious, he'll detach from any object that he was adhered to. It seems that it takes a conscious effort on Peter's part to cling to an object. In the same vein, he can't be "accidentally" stuck to an object. He's always in control of this power, unlike his spider-sense.

Spider-Man concentrates on using his hands or feet 90% of the time, but he can use this ability with any part of his body at any given time.

It seems that he truly can do all that a spider can.

Don't let the Green Goblin get too far ahead though. If he does, he'll launch another pair of Pumpkin Bombs at a bridge. As was the case earlier, you'll need to quickly repair the damage. The supports have small platforms that you can land on; swing in slowly and jump when you get near. You need to land so that you can shoot web at the supports, and there are no other places from which to shoot.

Once again, the Goblin flees the area. Chase him through the air high above a park and attack him. After you inflict even more damage, he runs off and Spider-Man chases after him to force a confrontation.

LEVEL DIFFICULTY

THE OFFER

PRIMARY OBJECTIVE

- Defeat the Green Goblin

BONUS OBJECTIVE

Deliver damage to Goblin quickly to get his Time Bonus; that's the only way to finish the level fast.

Ride Goblin. Get near him, hold jump, and try to land on him while you fall. If you can, you'll get this bonus.

GOLDEN SPIDER: YES   SECRET AREA: NO

STEP-BY-STEP SWINGTHROUGH

BOSS FIGHT

GREEN GOBLIN™

 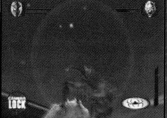

This is your first major fight with the Green Goblin, though not your last. Half of this fight takes place in the air, the other half on the ground. You begin above the city, locked on to your foe. Get in close for some physical attacks, or start with a barrage of Impact Webbing.

Once you connect with enough hits, the Green Goblin's Glider crashes through the roof of a nearby building. Follow his descent to the building and drop inside. The **Golden Spider** is located on one side of the room, so be sure to pick it up.

When Goblin crashes down into the first building, check the sides of the room to find Flip Mule. You'll probably spot it when you swing in, but make sure you pick it up before you leave.

CONTINUED

GOLDEN SPIDER

FLIP MULE . . . .**KICK KICK JUMP**

FLIP MULE COMBO

The Flip Mule does a good amount of damage, and places Spider-Man out of harm's upon completion. The final flip sends you over your target's head and past him a good distance. It can be useful for hurting one strong member in a pack of targets and getting away.

You need to hurt the Goblin enough in here to make him run again, and now is a good time to test out your new combo on him. Watch out for his flash grenades. If you get blinded, back off until you can see again.

AN OFFER YOU CAN REFUSE

The Green Goblin is obviously more than slightly insane, as he propositions Spider-Man to join him. Exactly what you'd do together is unknown. Rule a corporation in tights perhaps?

After the Goblin takes a few hits, he calls in his Glider again and takes off. Chase him out the door and get up in the air again. You need to knock him down once more, and he's not going to make it easy.

His Glider joins the fight now, firing at Spider-Man, adding to the Green Goblin's bombardment. You can quickly force him down though, and if you need it, there is a **Health Spider** on the buildings below.

After you knock him around a bit more, he dives to another rooftop, and drops down into the building. Chase him down and jump in, but grab some health if you aren't full.

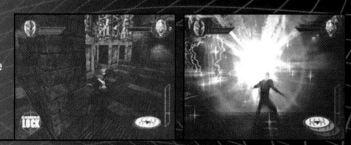

The room you land in has active electrical generators—be careful around their surges. If you have enough fluid, you can stay back and fire Impact Webs at the Goblin. If you don't, use one of Spider-Man's jumping combos to knock the Goblin down from a distance.

SPIDER-MAN'S™ BEST FRIENDS

If you need to recharge, check the top corners of the room, where there are Health Spiders and Web Fluid Spiders.

After you've dealt the Green Goblin enough knocks to the head, he calls his Glider for the final time, and flees. He takes off, but not before leaving Spider-Man with a decision to make: chase him or defuse the bombs he planted in the city.

THE GREEN GOBLIN™

The Green Goblin is Spider-Man's arch-enemy. Businessman Norman Osborn turns into this ghoulish persona after exposure to an experimental formula. The formula increases his intelligence and strength, but also drives him insane.

LEVEL DIFFICULTY 1 2 3 4 5

RACE AGAINST TIME

PRIMARY OBJECTIVE

● Defuse the bombs

BONUS OBJECTIVE

The Time Bonus on this level merges nicely with the main objective. If you use fast web swinging, you will probably get the objective every time.

GOLDEN SPIDER: NO   SECRET AREA: NO

STEP-BY-STEP SWINGTHROUGH

Although this is an extremely short level, it's a difficult one. Your task is to defuse the seven bombs placed on the various rooftops Of course, the timers make this task a bit more difficult. As the mission begins, jump from your starting position and swing for the rooftop straight ahead.

WHERE ARE THE BOMBS?

If you're having trouble locating the bombs, simply follow the Spider Compass. It will lead you directly to them.

Although the Hunter Killer drones are a distraction, avoid engaging in combat with them. You *must* focus on the bombs. When you land on the first rooftop, get close to the bomb and hit punch to disarm it. Turn ninety degrees to the right, jump, and start swinging for the building ahead.

The second bomb is located between the pair of buildings you're swinging towards. The bomb is located much higher than the first one, so you must gain altitude while you're swinging. Get inside the gap, defuse the bomb, then do an about-face and head for the third bomb.

WARNING At first, you only need to disarm one bomb in the time provided. Then it increases to two at once. Then the total is upped to *three* at once. Thankfully, you only need to disarm one bomb with the last timer.

Watch out for the spotlights while swinging. If you pass through them, you'll get blasted with gunfire. Land on the next rooftop and disarm the third bomb. After doing so, turn around again and take off, holding the Web Swing button to gain speed.

The fourth bomb is a good distance away, so pick up some speed while swinging. When you get within range, time your jump so that you release at the apex of your swing. When timed correctly, you can land right by the bomb. Disarm it, jump, and start swinging again.

The fifth bomb is located off to the left a bit, and it's not too far from the fourth bomb. Jump and land near it, disarm it, and then do an about-face and head off to the right.

If you continue to swing quickly, you can reach the sixth bomb with some time remaining. If you fail to move swiftly, you may not reach it at all. Hurry to disarm it, then jump and start swinging fast, slightly to the left.

The final bomb is a good distance from the sixth bomb. You need to quickly swing the entire way to reach it in time. After safely disarming the bombs, the mission ends.

KRAVEN'S™ TEST

LEVEL DIFFICULTY: 1 2 3 4 5

PRIMARY OBJECTIVE

● Escape Kraven's Traps

BONUS OBJECTIVE

None

GOLDEN SPIDER: NO

SECRET AREA: NO

STEP-BY-STEP SWINGTHROUGH

DIFFERENT VERSIONS

If you're playing the Xbox, you've got two additional levels to play through. PlayStation 2 and GameCube owners should skip ahead in the guide to *The Razor's Edge*.

This level is simple and straightforward, but challenging. Spider-Man immediately gets gassed by Kraven and gets poisoned. To escape the cloud, go through the door to your right, then continue right again in the hallway to get out.

Go through the sliding doors and down the steps into the exhibit hallways. Kraven has filled them with traps and you're going to have to dodge them all.

The masks will shoot flames, bear traps line the floor, stake traps will whip out at a moment's notice, and parts of the ceiling are covered with spikes as well. Navigate your way through carefully, jumping over the bear traps and jets of flame, while staying under the spikes in the ceiling.

KRAVEN™ THE HUNTER

Born of Russian descent, Kraven the Hunter is widely recognized for his hunting prowess.

During his time in the jungle, he met a witch doctor who'd created an herbal potion that enhanced the speed and strength of whoever drank it. Kraven didn't resist. He found that his strength increased and his speed increased as well, realizing that the jungle animals were no longer a challenge

Kraven soon learned of Spider-Man's existence. He recognized Spider-Man's power as soon as he saw him—he had found his new prey. Kraven became more and more interested in Spider-Man and began to focus on his hunt. Learning as much as he could about Spider-Man, Kraven fought him on several occasions. He truly was an amazing hunter.

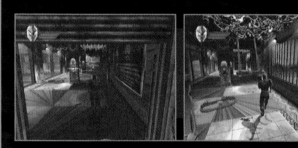

Around the first corner is a **Health Spider**. Beyond it, in the hall, more traps await—a swinging log, a swinging flaming weight, and an electrified wall. Evade them all and head through the door at the end.

There's only one new trick in this section: a rotating line of spikes on the ground. Avoid all the rest of the traps and get to the end of the hall—when you go through the exit door, you're going to come under fire.

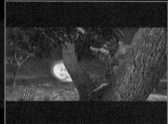

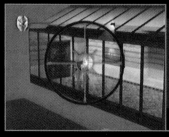

Kraven is waiting outside, watching the hall with a sniper rifle. The camera will shift to an external view; you need to guide Spider-Man down the hall, ducking behind the pillars when Kraven's crosshair appears.

Watch out for the flames in the next room, you don't want to get caught before you enter another exhibit hall. Proceed through the hall—now with flaming logs and a nasty mix of traps.

You're almost done. Head through another exhibit hall, this one with a **Health Spider** to replenish you near the beginning. Keep moving, avoiding the traps as you go.

Another open hall will have Kraven trying to snipe you once again. Evade him as you did before, ducking behind the pillars until you reach the next trap filled hallway.

There are **Health Spiders** in both of the next branches, you may need them with the traps here. Remember to take your time as you move. Studying the patterns will help you get through unscathed.

Once again, avoid Kraven's incoming bullets, run through the hall, and you'll finally reach the exit.

THE MIGHTY HUNTER

PRIMARY OBJECTIVE

- Defeat Kraven

BONUS OBJECTIVE

The Time Bonus is not a hard one to get, assuming you want to survive. Speed is important to come out of this level alive.

GOLDEN SPIDER: YES

SECRET AREA: YES

STEP-BY-STEP SWINGTHROUGH

BOSS FIGHT

KRAVEN THE HUNTER™

No one said Kraven fights fair when he's hunting. The poison that has afflicted Spider-Man will drain his health slowly, but steadily. You need to defeat Kraven quickly to survive this encounter. Head straight through the door to face Kraven's challenge.

WARNING Spider-Man's draining health is really bad news, particularly coupled with Kraven's strength potion. Defeating him quickly is the only option.

The room he has prepared is filled with flames and electricity, and there's a snake pit directly in front of you. Get on Kraven immediately, you need to put him down fast.

LEVEL DIFFICULTY 1 2 3 4 5

If you need health, drop into the snake pit (counter-intuitive admittedly), and grab the single **Health Spider** there. To get back out, go through the wall marked with a cobra; it will open up, letting you into the passages below the arena.

To get back out, go right, then up the ramp to the left. Don't take the first left turn, it leads down to a **Web Fluid Spider**, but the traps make it too costly of a venture.

Kraven will probably chase you down here; engage him if you're comfortable fighting in these close quarters. If you want to get away, just run out to return to the main room.

Farther down in the passages, if you don't exit through the ramp, is a medical room with **Health** and **Web Fluid Spiders** in it—don't go in unless you absolutely need the health. It is, unsurprisingly, a trap. The room will begin to fill with gas. To get out, go through the vent in the ceiling and work your way back to the arena.

SECRET AREA

Take a left turn in the vents to get this secret, along with the Golden Spider.

CONTINUED

GOLDEN SPIDER

HAYMAKER . . . . .KICK JUMP PUNCH

Fighting Kraven out in the main area is probably your best bet; use Spider-Man's agility to good effect, and back off when you need to.

Kraven will occasionally drink a potion, greatly increasing his speed and damage. Stay away from him while he's in this state, then retaliate when it wears off.

Keep the pressure on and Kraven will fall, his hunt ended. Defeated, he will give Spider-Man the antidote to the poison, and Spider-Man will leave him dangling for the police.

EXTRA DAMAGE

Use Advanced Web Gloves when you do get a chance to attack. You don't have much time and the extra damage will greatly decrease the number of hits you need to land.

LEVEL DIFFICULTY 1 2 3 4 5

THE RAZOR'S EDGE

PRIMARY OBJECTIVE

● Defeat 50 Razor Bats

BONUS OBJECTIVE

There's a Remaining Health Bonus on this level. Try to avoid taking too much damage. This isn't easy to do, because of the flock of Bats.

A No Power-Up Bonus will add to the difficulty. This task isn't easy, but it is possible to achieve if you can get into a good rhythm when destroying the Razor Bats.

GOLDEN SPIDER: NO

SECRET AREA: NO

STEP-BY-STEP SWINGTHROUGH

This level is even shorter than *Race Against Time* and seems to end in no time. You must destroy 50 Razor Bats to finish the level, which you can easily accomplish by using the right move.

What you need to do is lock the camera on a bat, swing through the entire flock, and press and hold the kick button. The Cannonball Kick will knock out a bunch of Razor Bats at once.

Continue to sweep back and forth through the cloud of Razor Bats to deplete their numbers. Eventually, the Green Goblin will drop off more for you to play with.

If your health gets low, check the nearby buildings for some **Health Spiders** and then get back to fighting. Although the Razor Bats aren't very dangerous during the actual combat, they can slice you to ribbons if you ignore them.

After defeating the fiftieth bat, Spider-Man realizes that chasing the Green Goblin isn't the thing to do now and instead seeks cover. This activates your Spider Compass, which points to a nearby unfinished construction site.

WEAPONS OF THE GREEN GOBLIN™

Razor Bats

The Green Goblin rarely uses these evil little weapons, but they can be deadly if used correctly. He's created boomerang-like weapons shaped like bats to carry on his Halloween-esque facade. They're made from a high density alloy and can rip through Spider-Man's webbing—or flesh.

Pumpkin Bombs

These are the Green Goblin's trademark weapons. Cast in the form of miniature jack-o-lanterns, these bombs are his most feared accessory. Over the years, he's created many different types. He commonly uses his incendiary and concussion grenade-like bombs, but he has been known to fill bombs with smoke or gas as well.

LEVEL DIFFICULTY
1 2 3 4 5

BREAKING AND ENTERING

PRIMARY OBJECTIVES

- Recover five pieces of the security code
- Use the code to exit the level

BONUS OBJECTIVE

Move quickly and use your Web Zip to get around while crawling on the ceiling to get the Time Bonus.

Don't get spotted! There's a Stealth Bonus to be had on this level.

GOLDEN SPIDER: YES   SECRET AREA: YES

STEP-BY-STEP SWINGTHROUGH

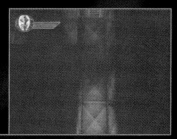

Using a little detective work on one of the broken Razor Bats that Peter recovered, it quickly becomes clear that the Green Goblin is involved with Oscorp. Knowing this, you must break into the building and recover five pieces of a code to penetrate deeper into the level. To get started, head through the vent for a short distance to reach a long hallway.

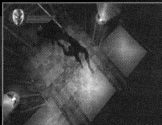

Upon entering the hallway, it becomes apparent that a stealthy approach is critical here. If a guard spots you and trips the alarm, a pack of android Super Soldiers will emerge and begin assaulting you. To avoid this scenario, stick to the ceiling and crawl to the end of the hallway.

FACIAL EXPRESSIONS

There's more to learn from one's face than simply their mood. The image of Spider-Man's face next to your Health and Web Fluid meters changes from fully lit to completely dark as you move through areas of shadow. If you are completely hidden, you can wait out an alarm until the Super Soldiers leave.

When you reach the very first room with a security camera in it, if you check the back, you'll find a set of elevators. You can activate the switches to open the doors, and enter to trigger a secret.

When you go through the door at the end of the hall, you'll enter a small foyer with some elevators at the back and a security camera to the left. Get onto the ceiling quickly. The door you need to enter is just under the security camera's watchful eye. Crawl just above the camera, wait for it to look away, then drop down and run through the door.

There's another security camera to the left of the small staircase, but you can avoid it. To do so, Web Zip to the ceiling, crawl forward, and then go through the door.

SPIDER-SNEAK

Yes, this mission is a bit different than previous ones, but it isn't very long. Just use a bit of patience to avoid being spotted.

Once again, immediately crawl onto the ceiling in this room. There are several computer terminals here, as well as a few guards and a security camera. The first piece of the code is here, as well as the **Golden Spider**. Wait for the guard to move away, then drop down to get them.

GOLDEN SPIDER

HIGH STOMP . . . . .KICK PUNCH JUMP

CODE BREAKING

To retrieve all five pieces of the code, you need to crawl around the rooms, drop down to the computers after the guards move away, and press punch in front of the computer. It takes time to download a piece of the code, so make sure you have plenty of time.

Remember the room in which you found the first piece of the code? Well, there's a ramp leading up to a landing in there. You must cross the landing over to the right to access another computer room, which contains two more pieces of the code. As noted earlier, watch for the guards before you drop to check the computers.

WARNING If a guard is running for no apparent reason—even if you didn't hear anything—seek cover. If the alarm sounds and you're hidden, things will calm down quickly.

Find the door near the back of the room with the pair of code pieces. Go through it to find another set of stairs. Web Zip up to enter the final computer room.

Watch out for the security camera when you enter the final room. Get up on the ceiling to avoid being spotted. This centrally located room contains the remaining pieces of the code. Watch out for the guard, drop down when the coast is clear, and retrieve both pieces.

After retrieving the final pieces, get through the blast doors. There is a double door near the front of the room that leads straight to the blast doors. Go through them, dodge the security camera, and enter the blast doors.

This room has nothing but a door barred with an energy barrier. How can you get through? Use the code, of course! Approach the panel next to the door and hit punch to input the code. Select a piece of the code and press punch to place it. To open the door, line up the pieces from blue to red so the circuit lines match up. There's no time limit, so you can try as often as needed to get it right.

CHEMICAL CHAOS

PRIMARY OBJECTIVE

- Destroy the Chemical Lab

BONUS OBJECTIVE

The Time Bonus is very tough to meet if you plan to employ a stealth technique as well. You might want to try an alarm-filled run through the level to get it.

GOLDEN SPIDER: YES   SECRET AREA: NO

STEP-BY-STEP SWINGTHROUGH

What's behind the sealed blast doors and the locked energy barrier? Why, it's Oscorp's Chemical Weapons division. This isn't a good thing, particularly since the Green Goblin gets his "toys" from here. It's up to you to shut down this operation. This mission involves stealth, so getting spotted is a bad thing. Go through the starting door and crawl onto the ceiling.

DESTROYING THE LAB

You meet a cooperative scientist at the start of the level, who fills you in on your objectives as you proceed through the level. Basically, you need to hit six switches to complete the level. This is easier said than done, however, as security is high and Super Soldiers loom everywhere.

SPIDER-SENSE TO THE RESCUE!

Spider-Man's spider-sense will warn of approaching guards throughout the level. Use this to your advantage if you have trouble seeing the entire area.

The next area has several dead ends, but there's only one spot you need to reach—the door on the opposite side that leads deeper into the lab. Take a moment to crawl around on the ceiling and observe the area. You can find a **Health Spider** and **Web Fluid Spiders** at the end of the corridors. Watch out for the central route in this room, as it has security cameras focused on the ceiling.

SPIDEY SENSE WILL WARN YOU OF NEARBY GUARDS.

AVOIDING THE CAMERAS

If you get spotted, take cover in one of the two full shadow areas on the ceiling. One is located right above the door you need to go through; the other is located above the Web Fluid Spider.

After scouting the area, get above the door and watch the security guard below. Pay close attention to his pattern. You need to drop down and run through just as he walks away. To open the door, you must hit the switch beside it so press punch as soon as you get near it.

BRUTE FORCE

It *is* possible to just run through this level, but it isn't easy. To do so, you must know the exact path to run and you need to dodge the Super Soldiers. Try it a few times if you don't like the stealth approach. Also, you can dodge and double jump to evade the Super Soldiers.

Next, you must navigate through a cycling series of laser trip-wires. You can either get on the wall and Web Zip past them, or stay on the ground and execute a diving roll.

The next security grid isn't too difficult. Crawl onto the wall and move up or down to avoid the tripwires. Upon reaching the end, check the ceiling for the **Golden Spider**.

GOLDEN SPIDER

PALM . . . . .KICK PUNCH KICK

GOLDEN SPIDER

HEAD HAMMER . . . .PUNCH JUMP PUNCH

Check the hall near the Golden Spider to find Control Rooms A and B. You must enter both rooms, flip the switches, and then go through the central door to reach the main Control Room. Once inside the main Control Room, flip the switch on the *right*. If you trigger the left one, it's game over!

TIMING IS CRUCIAL

As you drop down to enter Control Rooms A and B, remember to allow for the extra time it takes to open the door. You don't want to get spotted just outside your objectives.

After flipping the switch, return to the door directly below the area in which you grabbed the Golden Spider and go through it. Keep an eye on the security cameras and the security grid. You need to exit the room undetected.

SPOTTED!

If you get spotted, you can hide in the dark corner in the room.

There's a dark corner in one part of the room and a **Health Spider** in the other. Use them both if needed, then exit through the door *not* used by the Super Soldiers.

You now face a wall of laser tripwires. Stand just inside the door, wait for a gap between the tripwires to appear, and then roll through.

This is where Control Rooms C and D are located. Make sure you enter Control Room C first. There's a **Health Spider** in the back hallway, and a **Web Fluid Spider** in the only other room in this area.

When you're ready, try to enter Control Room D—it's locked! Unfortunately, the head researcher has the key. To get it, hop onto the ceiling and wait for him to appear. When he does, drop down and pound the key out of him, then quickly enter and flip the switch.

You're almost done! Return to the central room (between Control Rooms A and B), and flip the left switch this time. Oscorp's Chemical Weapons plans just went down the drain, so you're done here.

TO STEALTH, OR NOT TO STEALTH?

There's no need to worry about a stealth approach on the way back unless, of course, you're low on health.

OSCORP'S ULTIMATE WEAPON

PRIMARY OBJECTIVES

- Destroy the 10 Generators
- Destroy the Sensor Array

BONUS OBJECTIVE

Defeat the Super Mech quickly to escape and get this Time Bonus.

GOLDEN SPIDER: NO   **SECRET AREA: NO**

STEP-BY-STEP SWINGTHROUGH

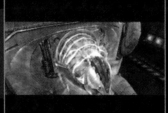

If you're a giant corporation, what do you spend your shareholders money on? How about a gigantic, multi-ton giant robot with a huge laser cannon? You start the level swinging, with incoming fire coming from Hunter Killer drones and the gigantic Super Mech.

This level is essentially an aerial combat mission. To disable the Super Mech, you must destroy its 10 generators. Four generators are located on the wall in front of it, two are directly in front of it, and four more are on its back.

Focus your attention on the four generators on the opposite wall. Swing near them, activate Camera Lock, and fire Impact Webbing at them. You don't want to land, because you'll take too much damage from incoming fire.

WARNING

When you're out in front of the Super Mech, it will power up the giant energy cannon on its right arm and bombard Spider-Man. If you get close to the cannon, however, the mech can't target you.

While you're swinging around, check below the catwalks in the area for some power-ups. You can find **Health** and **Web Fluid Spiders**.

After you destroy the four frontal generators, get close to the Super Mech's face and destroy the two generators just below it.

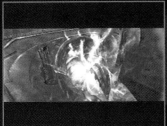 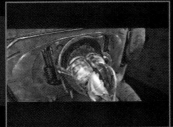

Next, focus your attack on the four generators on the Super Mech's back. It's actually easier to get these compared to the ones in the front, because you'll see less incoming fire.

TARGETING PROBLEMS?

The fighting here may get frustrating when using Camera Lock, because it will sometimes lock onto the Hunter Killer drones on occasion. If this happens, change targets while swinging near the generators. You will eventually lock onto the right target.

After destroying all the generators, just land behind the Super Mech's head and destroy the Sensor Array. Swing over it, drop down, and unleash a combo or two; it doesn't take much to destroy it. When it blows up, the Super Mech goes down with it.

ESCAPE FROM OSCORP

PRIMARY OBJECTIVE

- Escape from Oscorp

BONUS OBJECTIVE

Defeat the Super Soldiers. This is *not* an easy bonus objective. In fact, it's probably one of the most difficult. You must decide if getting a few extra points is worth facing a mob of angry androids.

GOLDEN SPIDER: YES   SECRET AREA: NO

STEP-BY-STEP SWINGTHROUGH

You must get out of the building. The whole area is alerted to Spider-Man's presence now, and the Super Soldiers are out in force. You should recognize this area, though; it's Breaking and Entering. This time, however, you enter from the blast doors. First stop, the **Golden Spider** directly in front of your starting position.

GOLDEN SPIDER

ADVANCED IMPACT WEB (ENHANCED MODE ONLY)

In enhanced mode, if you check the dead end exit (that is, go through the WRONG energy door), you can find Advanced Impact Web.

GOLDEN SPIDER

HAYMAKER . . . . .KICK JUMP PUNCH

ALERT!

During your first visit to this area, you needed to take it slow. This time, you need to do the exact opposite. Swing fast, Web Zip, jump and run! The barrage of fire from the Super Soldiers will cut you down if you don't finish this level fast.

To get out you need to get past a variety of things, including: the laser barrier, the sentry cannons, and the Super Soldiers. You must first disarm the sentry cannons. To do so, go down the landing to the right and enter the door at the end of the hall. The control panel shuts down the sentry cannons.

After disabling the cannons, return to the landing and run down to the opposite side to find another control panel room. Hit this switch to disable the laser barrier, which opens your escape route.

Now swing over the computer area to find the exit door. Unfortunately, a energy barrier blocks your escape. Check the floor to find a line of power leading away from it to a switch nearby. To exit the room, flip the switch to disable the barrier.

WARNING

Remember that there are two identical computer areas, and both have doors that you can open. However, one is a red herring. The correct one is the door closest to the control room that disabled the security cameras.

Drop down the stairs and go through the door to the small foyer you came through before. Destroy the Super Soldier, and flip the switch on the sealed door. It takes a few seconds for the door to open, so if any more Super Soldiers rush you, web them up.

As soon as the door opens, dash through it and start swinging! The hallway is filled with Super Soldiers, so avoid getting caught in the crossfire. To escape from Oscorp, you need to reach the end of the hallway.

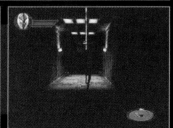

MARY JANE KIDNAPPED

PRIMARY OBJECTIVE

● Catch Green Goblin

BONUS OBJECTIVE

None

GOLDEN SPIDER: NO

SECRET AREA: NO

STEP-BY-STEP SWINGTHROUGH

You knew it would eventually occur—the Green Goblin has kidnapped Mary Jane! When you begin this aerial pursuit level, you're already locked onto the Green Goblin and he's trying to flee as fast as his Glider will take him.

Don't let up, because the Green Goblin's Glider is very fast. Even when swinging at full speed, there are some areas in the level in which he'll pull away from you.

Watch out for floating bombs that the Green Goblin drops. To avoid them, get some altitude and stay above the whole mess. Be careful, though, when heading for a group of buildings; you don't want to lose sight of him.

THE GREEN GOBLIN'S™ GLIDER

Though relatively small, the Goblin Glider can carry up to 400 pounds. Its vertical-thrust ability makes it extremely maneuverable and it can maintain speeds of up to 90 miles per hour. A miniature turbo-fan gives it its speed and power.

With metal stirrups mounted on the wings, the Green Goblin can fly on the glider leaving his hands free to toss pumpkin bombs or electrocute his enemies. In addition, the glider is voice-activated and responds to commands from the Green Goblin as if he were manually handling the controls. Using these voice controls, the Green Goblin doesn't even need to be on the glider to command it.

To finish off the fearsome facade, the Green Goblin equipped the glider with a horned head to ram things with. Unfortunately, while in a battle with Spider-Man, the Green Goblin found out what it was like to be on the receiving end of the ram.

In a few places the Green Goblin quickly gains altitude, which may cause you to swing into a building. When this occurs, release the Web Swing button or execute a quick web break by jumping and then swinging again. You need the added maneuverability to quickly rise up.

You must stay close to him, because this level is a bit longer than the previous chases. However, the Green Goblin doesn't have any more tricks to pull when you finally catch up with him. It's time for the final showdown.

FACE-OFF AT THE BRIDGE

PRIMARY OBJECTIVES

- Defeat the Green Goblin!
- Save Mary Jane

BONUS OBJECTIVE

None

GOLDEN SPIDER: NO   **SECRET AREA: NO**

STEP-BY-STEP SWINGTHROUGH

BOSS FIGHT

GREEN GOBLIN™

This is it; the final confrontation with the Green Goblin. It's time to put an end to his insanity. Before the fight with the Goblin begins, though, you must help Mary Jane. She's on top of the bridge, just ahead of where you start the level.

Land near this location (see screenshot), pick up Mary Jane, and then jump off the edge and swing down to safely place her on the spider symbol. You may need to move her if the Goblin begins to attack her.

When Mary Jane is safe, focus on the green menace flying above. Activate Camera Lock and take to the skies. You must pummel him until he lands on the bridge below.

After knocking the Green Goblin off his glider, head to the ground and let him have it! Watch out for his glider, though, because it will continue to attack while you fight the Goblin.

LOW ON HEALTH?

If you're low on health or web fluid, check out the bridge. You'll find these items scattered around the area.

After causing a decent amount of damage, the Green Goblin hops back on his glider. It's time to chase him again! Just repeat the process: smack the Goblin around some more until he lands again.

DEALIN' DAMAGE

Try to land quickly and put on Advanced Web Gloves. If successful, you can inflict some massive damage to Goblin as soon as he hits the ground!

Continue to knock the Goblin out of the air if he takes off, and then pummel him on the ground when the chance arises. After defeating the Green Goblin, your work is done. Enjoy the ending!

YOUR FRIENDLY NEIGHBORHOOD TRAVEL GUIDE

THIS SECTION WAS DESIGNED FOR YOU GAMERS THAT SIMPLY WANT A GLIMPSE AT THE LEVEL WITHOUT BEING GIVEN ALL THE INSIGHTS AND STRATEGIES INCLUDED IN THE STEP-BY-STEP SWINGTHROUGH. LISTED IN THIS SECTION IS A SUMMARY OF THE OBJECTIVES, WHAT YOU NEED TO GET, AND MAPS THAT WILL SHOW YOU HOW TO GET TO THE LOCATION. GOOD LUCK!

SEARCH FOR JUSTICE

PRIMARY OBJECTIVES
- Find out who Killed your Uncle
- Locate the Killer

BONUS OBJECTIVE
- Find and Defeat all of the Thugs

ENEMY PRESENCE
- Moderate

GOLDEN SPIDER
- Yes

SECRET AREA
- Yes

WAREHOUSE HUNT

PRIMARY OBJECTIVE
- Find Uncle Ben's Killer

BONUS OBJECTIVE
- Stealth

ENEMY PRESENCE
- High

GOLDEN SPIDER
- Yes

SECRET AREA
- Yes

BIRTH OF A HERO

PRIMARY OBJECTIVE
- Defeat Uncle Ben's Killer

BONUS OBJECTIVE
- Time

ENEMY PRESENCE
- High

GOLDEN SPIDER
- Yes

SECRET AREA
- Yes

OSCORP'S GAMBIT

PRIMARY OBJECTIVE
- Get some Pictures for Jonah

BONUS OBJECTIVE
- Destroy the Hunter Killer Drones

ENEMY PRESENCE
- Low

GOLDEN SPIDER
- No

SECRET AREA
- No

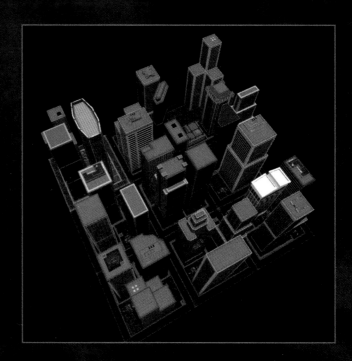

THE SUBWAY STATION

PRIMARY OBJECTIVE
- Protect Civilians

BONUS OBJECTIVE
- Time

ENEMY PRESENCE
- Low

GOLDEN SPIDER
- Yes

SECRET AREA
- No

LEVEL DIFFICULTY
1 . 2 . 3 . 4 . 5

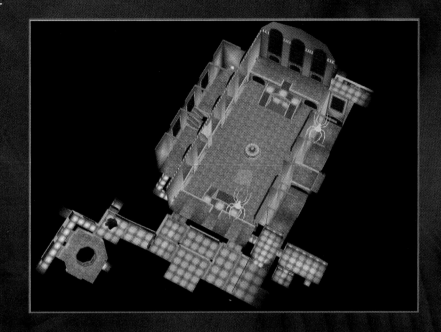

CHASE THROUGH THE SEWER

PRIMARY OBJECTIVE
- Catch up with the Shocker

BONUS OBJECTIVES
- Time
- Defeat all of the Thugs

ENEMY PRESENCE
- High

GOLDEN SPIDER
- Yes

SECRET AREA
- Yes

LEVEL DIFFICULTY
1 . 2 . 3 . 4 . 5

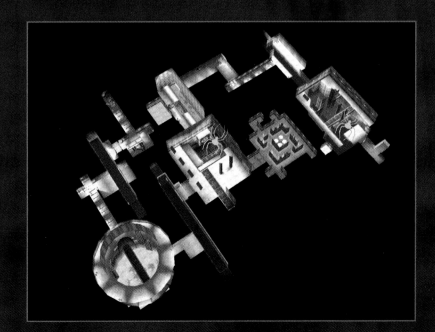

SHOWDOWN WITH THE SHOCKER™

LEVEL DIFFICULTY
1
2
3
4
5

PRIMARY OBJECTIVE
- Defeat the Shocker

BONUS OBJECTIVE
- Time

ENEMY PRESENCE
- Boss

GOLDEN SPIDER
- Yes

SECRET AREA
- Yes

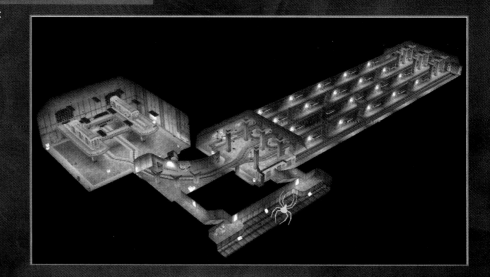

VULTURE'S™ LAIR

LEVEL DIFFICULTY
1
2
3
4
5

PRIMARY OBJECTIVE
- Ascend Vulture's Tower

BONUS OBJECTIVE
- Time

ENEMY PRESENCE
- High (If you count explosives)

GOLDEN SPIDER
- Yes

SECRET AREA
- No

VULTURE™ ESCAPES

PRIMARY OBJECTIVES
- Catch the Vulture
- Protect Civilians from his Attacks

BONUS OBJECTIVES
- Time
- Stay Close to the Vulture at all times

ENEMY PRESENCE
- Low

GOLDEN SPIDER
- No

SECRET AREA
- No

LEVEL DIFFICULTY 1 2 3 4 5

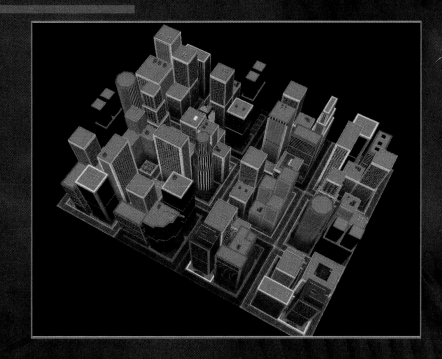

AIR DUEL WITH VULTURE™

PRIMARY OBJECTIVE
- Defeat the Vulture

BONUS OBJECTIVE
- Time

ENEMY PRESENCE
- Boss

GOLDEN SPIDER
- Yes

SECRET AREA
- No

LEVEL DIFFICULTY 1 2 3 4 5

CORRALLED

PRIMARY OBJECTIVES
- Protect the Scorpion
- Destroy the Spider Slayers

BONUS OBJECTIVE
- Keep the Scorpion Healthy

ENEMY PRESENCE
- Moderate

GOLDEN SPIDER
- Yes

SECRET AREA
- Yes

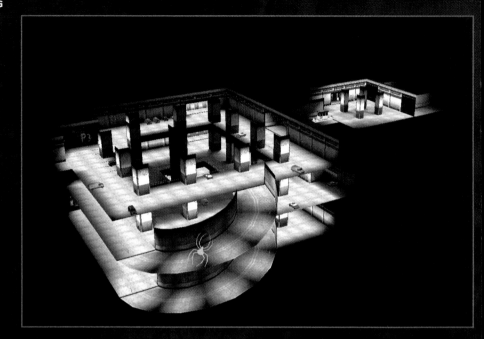

SCORPION'S™ REVENGE

PRIMARY OBJECTIVE
- Defeat the Scorpion

BONUS OBJECTIVE
- Don't use any Health or Web Fluid Spiders

ENEMY PRESENCE
- None

GOLDEN SPIDER
- Yes

SECRET AREA
- No

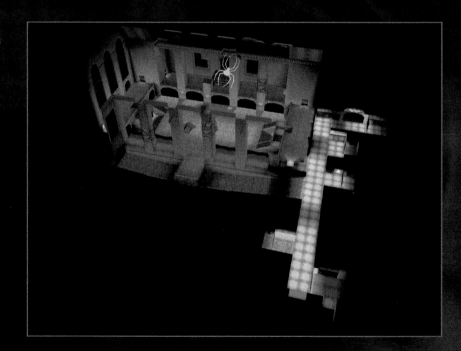

COUP D'ETAT

PRIMARY OBJECTIVES
● Save Mary Jane
● Chase the Green Goblin

BONUS OBJECTIVE
● Time

ENEMY PRESENCE
● None

GOLDEN SPIDER
● Yes

SECRET AREA
● No

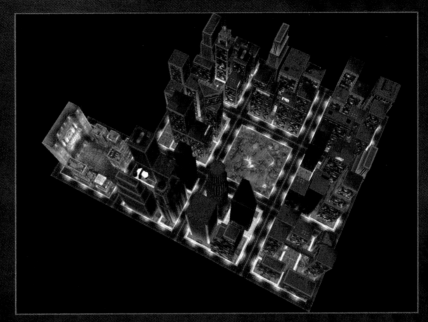

THE OFFER

PRIMARY OBJECTIVE
● Defeat the Green Goblin

BONUS OBJECTIVES
● Time
● Land on the Green Goblin's Glider in mid air

ENEMY PRESENCE
● Boss

GOLDEN SPIDER
● Yes

SECRET AREA
● No

RACE AGAINST TIME

PRIMARY OBJECTIVE
- Defuse the Bombs

BONUS OBJECTIVE
- Time

ENEMY PRESENCE
- Moderate

GOLDEN SPIDER
- No

SECRET AREA
- No

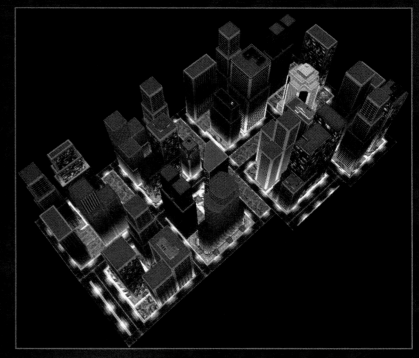

KRAVEN'S™ TEST

PRIMARY OBJECTIVE
- Escape Kraven's Traps

BONUS OBJECTIVE
- None

ENEMY PRESENCE
- None

GOLDEN SPIDER
- No

SECRET AREA
- No

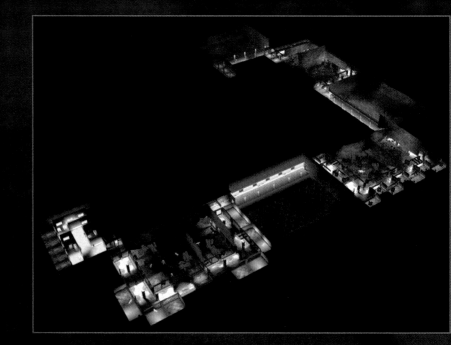

THE MIGHTY HUNTER

PRIMARY OBJECTIVE
- Defeat Kraven

BONUS OBJECTIVE
- Time

ENEMY PRESENCE
- None

GOLDEN SPIDER
- Yes

SECRET AREA
- Yes

THE RAZOR'S EDGE

PRIMARY OBJECTIVE
- Defeat 50 Razor Bats

BONUS OBJECTIVES
- Have a lot of Health when you Finish the Level
- Don't use any Health or Web Fluid Spiders

ENEMY PRESENCE
- High

GOLDEN SPIDER
- No

SECRET AREA
- No

BREAKING AND ENTERING

LEVEL DIFFICULTY 1 2 3 4 5

PRIMARY OBJECTIVES
- Recover Five Pieces of the Security Code
- Use the Code to Exit the Level

BONUS OBJECTIVES
- Time
- Stealth

ENEMY PRESENCE
- Low

GOLDEN SPIDER
- Yes

SECRET AREA
- Yes

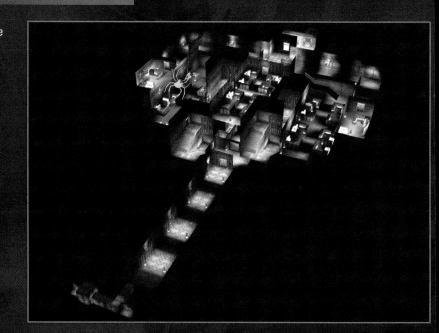

CHEMICAL CHAOS

LEVEL DIFFICULTY 1 2 3 4 5

PRIMARY OBJECTIVE
- Destroy the Chemical Lab

BONUS OBJECTIVE
- Time

ENEMY PRESENCE
- Low

GOLDEN SPIDER
- Yes

SECRET AREA
- No

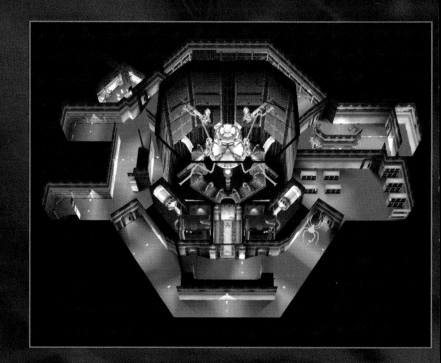

OSCORP'S ULTIMATE WEAPON

PRIMARY OBJECTIVES
- Destroy 10 Generators
- Destroy the Sensor Array

BONUS OBJECTIVE
- Time

ENEMY PRESENCE
- Low

GOLDEN SPIDER
- No

SECRET AREA
- No

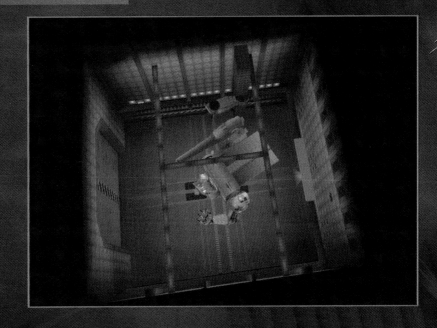

ESCAPE FROM OSCORP

PRIMARY OBJECTIVE
- Escape from Oscorp

BONUS OBJECTIVE
- Defeat all of the Super Soldiers

ENEMY PRESENCE
- High

GOLDEN SPIDER
- Yes

SECRET AREA
- No

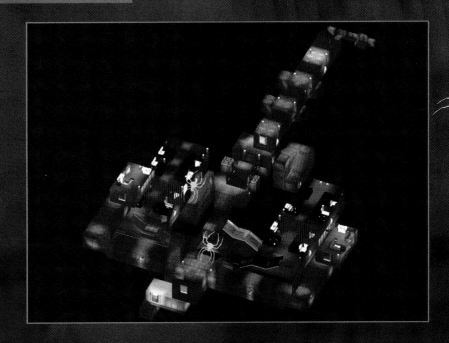

MARY JANE KIDNAPPED

LEVEL DIFFICULTY
1 2 3 4 5

PRIMARY OBJECTIVE
- Catch the Green Goblin

BONUS OBJECTIVE
- None

ENEMY PRESENCE
- None

GOLDEN SPIDER
- No

SECRET AREA
- No

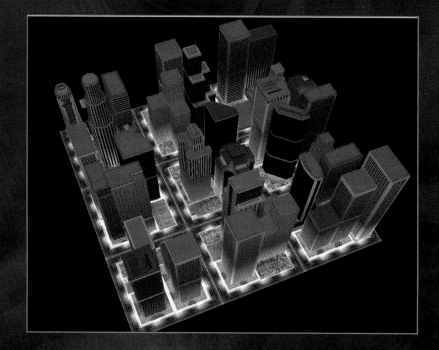

FACE-OFF AT THE BRIDGE

LEVEL DIFFICULTY
1 2 3 4 5

PRIMARY OBJECTIVES
- Defeat the Green Goblin
- Save Mary Jane

BONUS OBJECTIVE
- None

ENEMY PRESENCE
- Boss

GOLDEN SPIDER
- No

SECRET AREA
- No

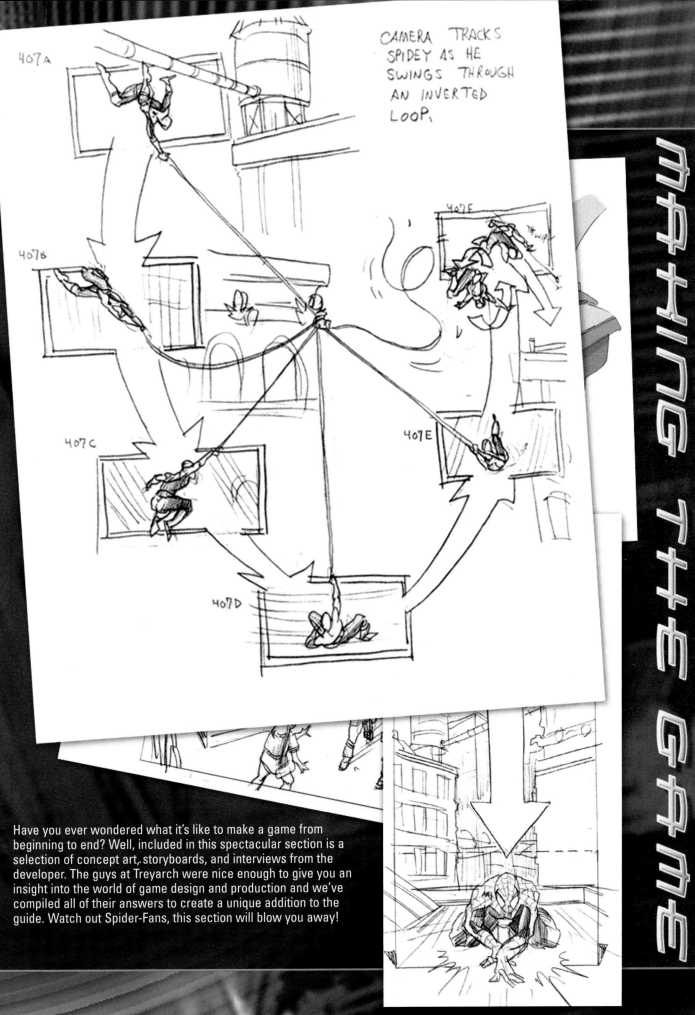

407A

CAMERA TRACKS SPIDEY AS HE SWINGS THROUGH AN INVERTED LOOP.

407B

407F

407C

407E

407D

Have you ever wondered what it's like to make a game from beginning to end? Well, included in this spectacular section is a selection of concept art, storyboards, and interviews from the developer. The guys at Treyarch were nice enough to give you an insight into the world of game design and production and we've compiled all of their answers to create a unique addition to the guide. Watch out Spider-Fans, this section will blow you away!

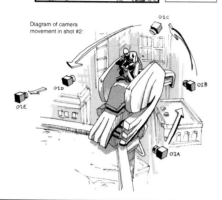

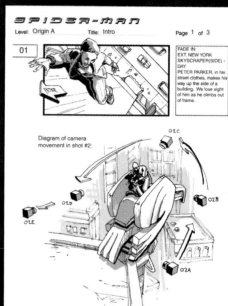

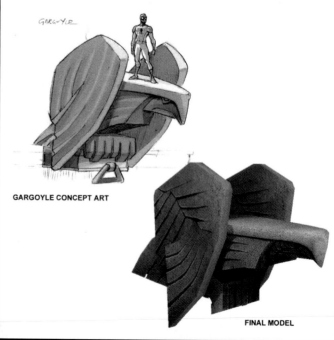

GARGOYLE CONCEPT ART

FINAL MODEL

CHOP SHOP

BIG STORAGE

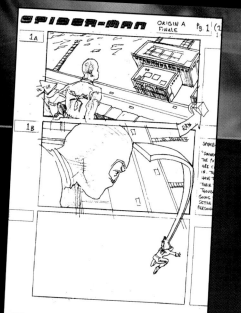

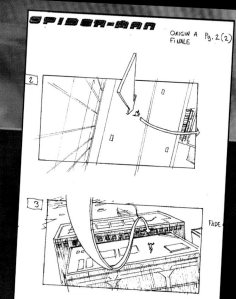

Boss Room

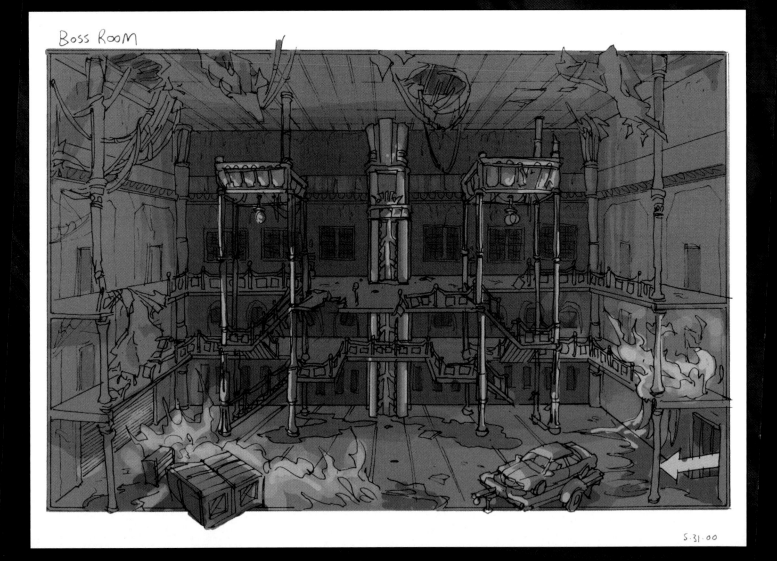

5.31.00

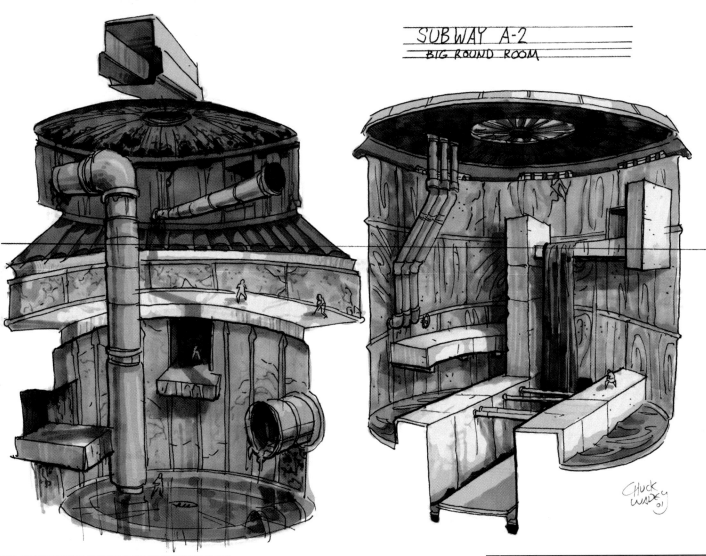

SUBWAY A-2
BIG ROUND ROOM

CHUCK WADEY 01

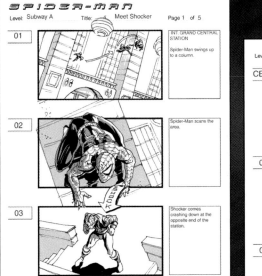

SPIDER-MAN

Level: Subway A   Title: Meet Shocker   Page 1 of 5

01 — INT. GRAND CENTRAL STATION

Spider-Man swings up to a column.

02 — Spider-Man scans the area.

03 — Shocker comes crashing down at the opposite end of the station.

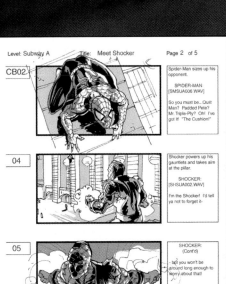

Level: Subway A   Title: Meet Shocker   Page 2 of 5

CB02 — Spider-Man sizes up his opponent.

SPIDER-MAN:
[SMSUA006.WAV]

So you must be...Quilt Man? Padded Pete? Mr. Triple-Ply? Oh! I've got it! "The Cushion!"

04 — Shocker powers up his gauntlets and takes aim at the pillar.

SHOCKER:
[SHSUA002.WAV]

I'm the Shocker! I'd tell ya not to forget it–

05 — SHOCKER:
(Cont'd)

– but you won't be around long enough to worry about that!

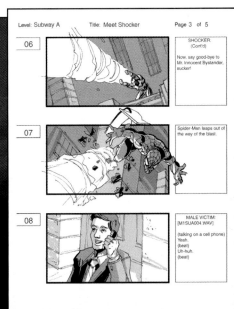

Level: Subway A   Title: Meet Shocker   Page 3 of 5

06 — SHOCKER:
(Cont'd)

Now, say good-bye to Mr. Innocent Bystander, sucker!

07 — Spider-Man leaps out of the way of the blast.

08 — MALE VICTIM:
[M1SUA004.WAV]

(talking on a cell phone)
Yeah.
(beat)
Uh-huh.
(beat)

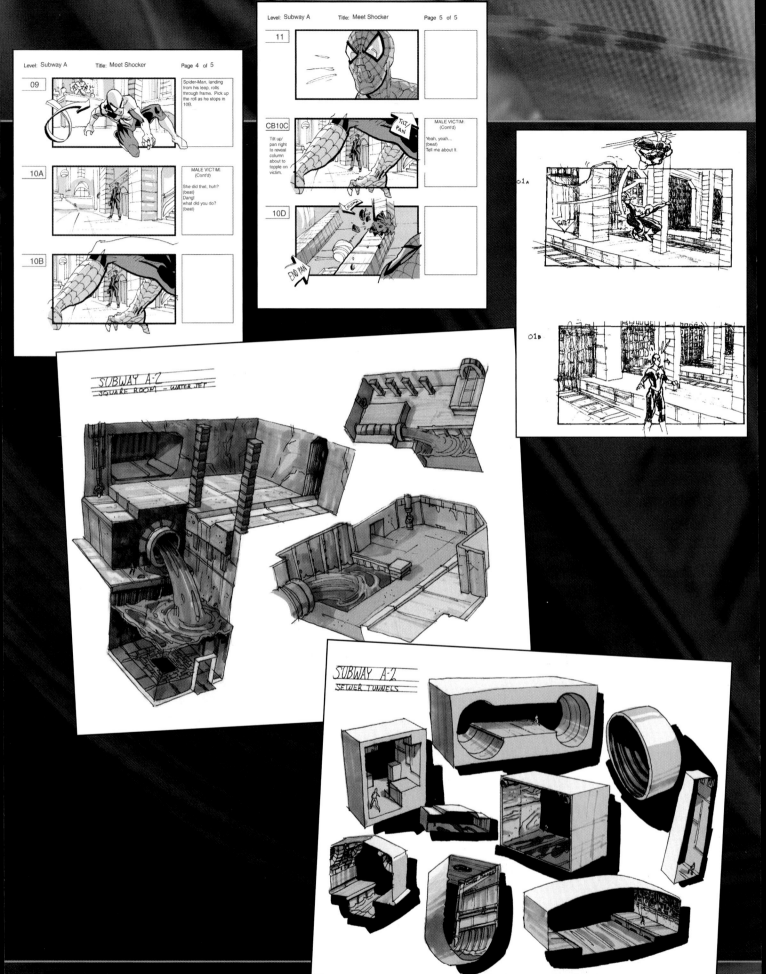

09

10A

MALE VICTIM:
(Cont'd)

She did that, huh?
(beat)
Dang!
what did you do?
(beat)

10B

11

CB10C

Tilt up/
pan right
to reveal
column
about to
topple on
victim.

TILT
PAN

MALE VICTIM:
(Cont'd)

Yeah, yeah...
(beat)
Tell me about it.

10D

END PAN

Spider-Man, landing
from his leap, rolls
through frame. Pick up
the roll as he stops in
10B.

O1A

GATE

O1B

SUBWAY A-2
SQUARE ROOM - WATER JET

SUBWAY A-2
SEWER TUNNELS

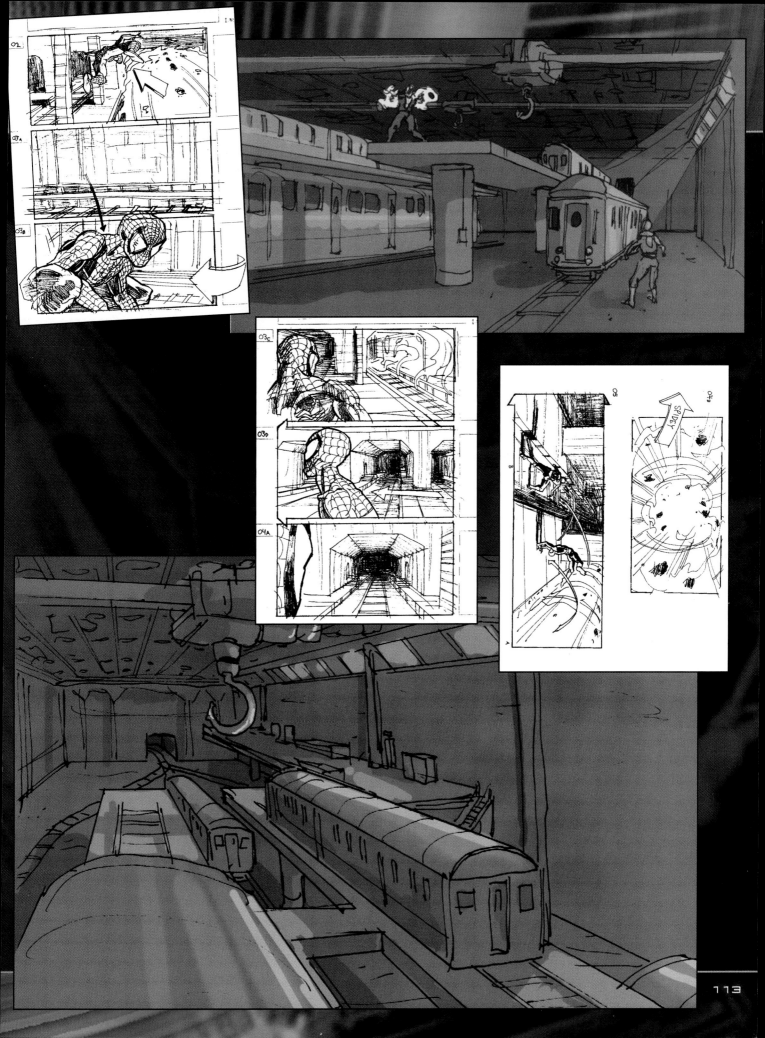

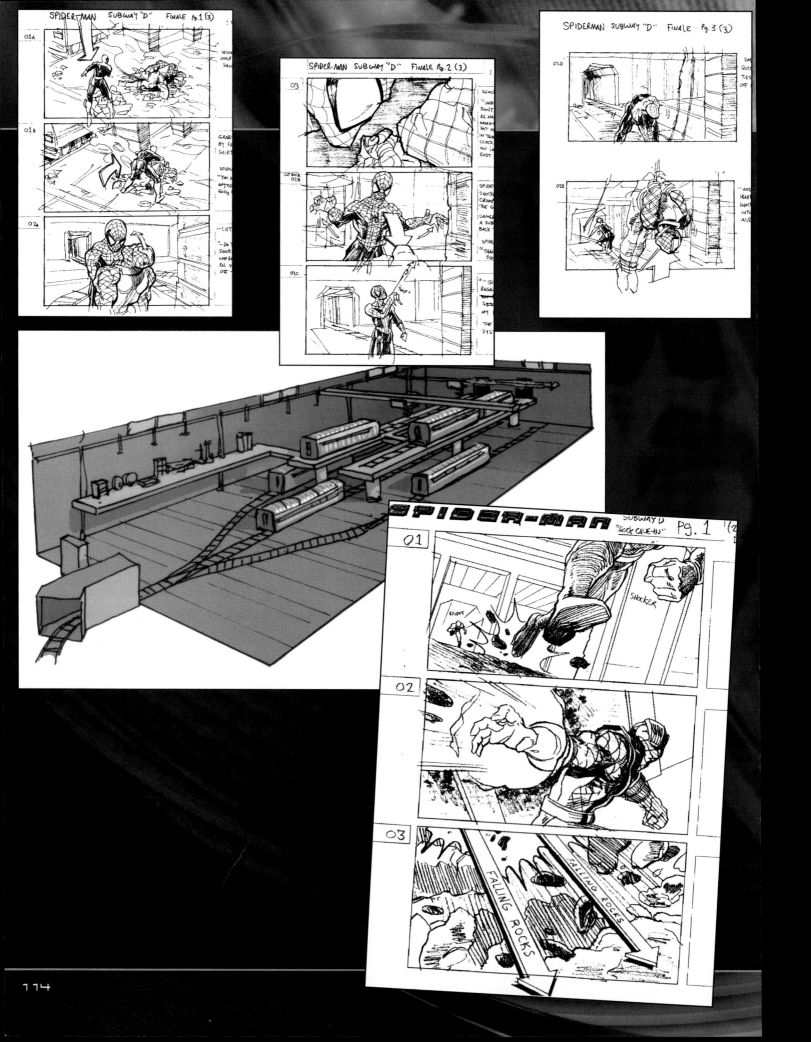

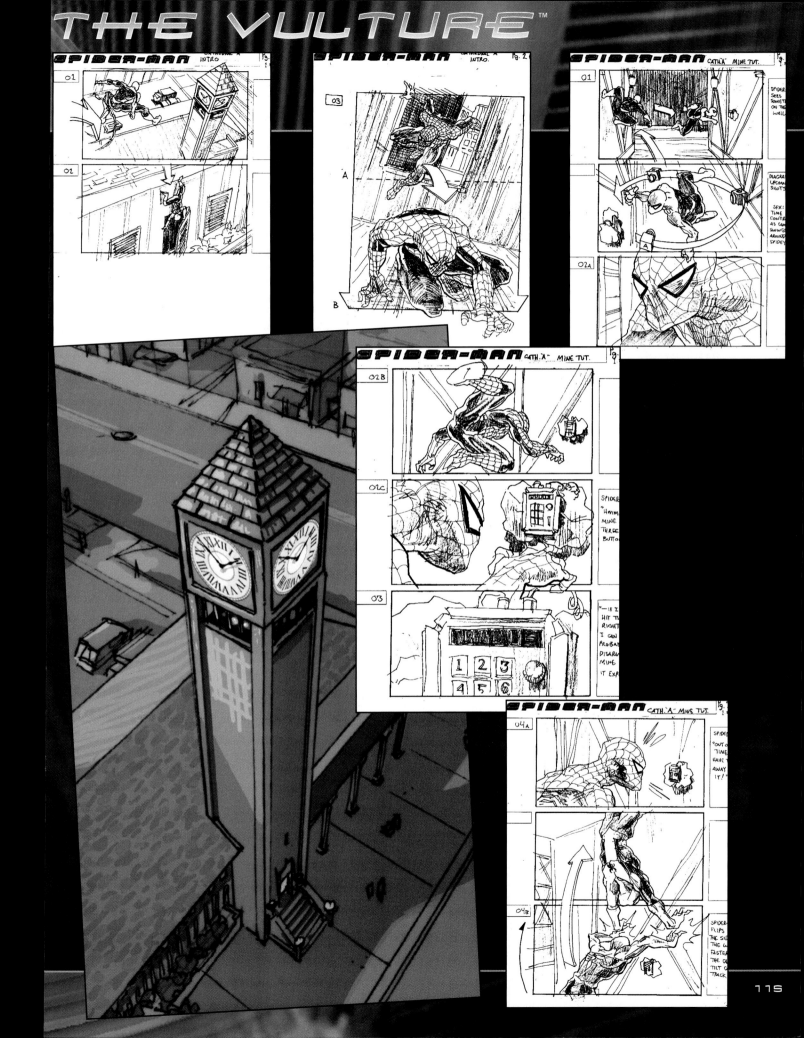

CATHEDRAL A
VULTURE'S WORKSHOP

Chuck
Wadey
01

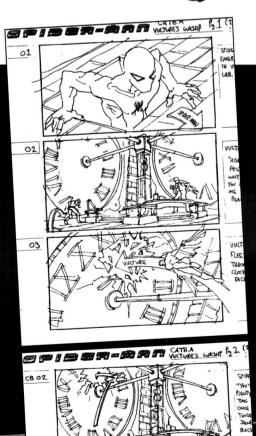

SPIDER-MAN
CATH. B FINALE

1

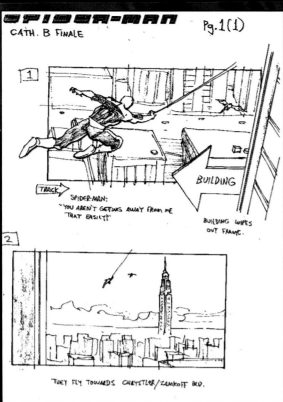

TRACK

SPIDER-MAN:
"YOU AREN'T GETTING AWAY FROM ME
THAT EASILY!"

BUILDING

BUILDING WIPES
OUT FRAME.

2

THEY FLY TOWARDS CHRYSTLER/ZAMKOFF BLD.

SPIDER-MAN

Level: Cathedral C   Scene: Outro   Page 1 of 1

01

ACTION
Spider-Man stands next to webbed-up Vulture.

DIALOGUE
(SM) Now Vulture, you can't go around taking things that don't belong to you.

02

ACTION

DIALOGUE
(SM) What kind of example does it set for impressionable youngsters out there?

FADE TO BLACK

FADE UP FROM BLACK

03

ACTION
Officer Smith holds bag of jewels as he talks to dangling Vulture.

DIALOGUE
(Smith) C'mon old timer...wouldn't want you falling before we can book you, right? Heh heh.

SPIDERMAN M3C FINAL CUTSCENE   Pg. 1 (3)

AFTER VULTURE'S DEFEAT, SPIDEY STANDS OVER HOLDING THE BAG OF JEWELS.

1) SPIDEY: "I BEEN OVER THIS WITH YOU BEFORE, VULTURE. YOU CAN'T GO AROUND TAKING THINGS THAT DON'T BELONG TO YOU."

A

B

C

"WHAT KIND OF EXAMPLE DOES IT SET FOR IMPRESSIONABLE YOUNGSTERS OUT THERE? SWEESH."

WHIP
PAN
UP

CREATIVE DIRECTOR CHRIS SOARES

HOBBIES: *I collect odd things like skulls and insects, but mostly I like playing with my kid.*

MAJOR TITLES WORKED ON: *Sid Meier's Civilization, Pirates Gold, Die by the Sword, Draconus - Cult of the Wyrm, Max Steel.*

FAVORITE FOOD TO SNACK ON WHILE GAMING: *Blue M&M's*

FAVORITE MOVIE: *Just one?!? "Delicatessen," "Train Spotting," "Pulp Fiction," "Blade Runner," "Alien," the list goes on and on.*

MOST RECENT GAME OBSESSION: *I work too much to really let myself get sucked into a great game, but I guess it was SSX. I'm really looking forward to diving into Metal Gear 2 now that our project has wrapped.*

Q: What was your specific role in the Spider-Man project? Or, what did your day-to-day tasks include?

A: *My role on the team was to provide the vision for the look and feel of the game. I worked as a liaison between Sony/Columbia TriStar and the Treyarch team and my role included organizing the massive amount of movie-related reference materials - concept art, photography from the set, swatches of cloth from the costumes, blueprints of the sets, etc. Then, I directed the team in creating a game that shared the same vision as Sam Raimi, the film's director.*

Q: How did the voiceover (VO) work take place? What involvement did you have in the process?

A: *All of the final voiceover (VO) was recorded at Woodholly Studios in Hollywood. Sergio, our audio director, Matt Rhoades, our writer, and myself selected the voice talent from a ton of submissions from talent agencies. On a few cases, we ended up going with people we worked with before like Dwight Schultz (Vulture) and Peter Lurie (Kraven).*

Q: Aside from Tobey Maguire, who else was involved?

A: *Willem Dafoe and Bruce Campbell, both from the feature film. Additional talent includes Josh Keaton, Jay Gordon, Cat O'Connor, Mike McColl and Michael Beattie. I should also mention the awesome crew at Woodholly.*

Q: At what point does the voiceover work happen in the project?

A: *We felt it was very important to put VO into the game early in the process, but we have also found it useful to utilize placeholder VO beforehand because it helps see how things will play out. In this instance, the catch was that big name actors like Tobey (Maguire) and Willem (Dafoe) cannot drop by every couple of weeks to do a few new lines so we recorded some of our team members as the characters in order to iron out any issues before the actors got involved. Although I read for a lot of the characters, I think the team will always remember Alex Bortoluzzi, our lead level builder's, rendition of Kraven, it was hilarious and awesome.*

Q: One of the coolest additions to the game is Bruce Campbell's voiceover work on the tutorial sections. How did he come to be a part of the project?

A: *Many game tutorials are notoriously dull, so we decided to add a lot more depth to Spider-Man's so players will enjoy learning all of his new moves as well as the basics. Whose voice is better than Bruce's with his wry delivery and sarcastic wit to liven up a tutorial?*

Q: Were there any restrictions concerning Spider-Man that you had to adhere to?

A: *It was clear from the beginning that this was the movie version of Spider-Man, not the comic book version, so we had to be very careful about adding any elements from the Marvel universe. We made the decision to add classic Marvel villains into the story line, because the movie only has the Green Goblin and one villain in a two-hour film won't give gamers the extended gameplay necessary in a video game. Therefore, because both the movie and the game focus on Spider-Man's origin story, we picked classic villains from early in Spider-Man's history. We presented this idea to both Sam Raimi and Marvel and they were supportive of our ideas, which was great!*

Q: After completing the game, what do you expect/want people to say about the gaming experience?

A: *I guess my hope would be they say something like, "Wow, that's the best super hero game I have ever played. They really nailed what it feels like to be Spider-Man."*

Q: The cinematic sequences in the game are incredible. How long did it take to make the cinemas? What is involved in creating them? Which one is your favorite and why?

A: *Thanks. I think it's important not to stop the flow of the game too often, but I did want to reward the players with some treats as they play though the game. Both Jon Lauf and Tim Smilovitch, who have backgrounds in creating 3D animation for television, handled the lion's share of the work on the cinematic sequences. All of the movies were done with Discreet's 3D Studio MAX and rendered on our render farm. We use Adobe's After Effects, Premiere and Photoshop for the other aspects like compositing, editing and texture maps. The entire process begins with a great script that is broken out into storyboards. We then create an animatic, which is rough animation with scratch audio, to see how it cuts and if the storytelling is coming though as planned. This is also a time in production when assets like the character models and the environments are created. Most of the movies were completed in the sense of a first pass until the final VO was recorded, then we did the final pass of lip sync and character animation. Players can unlock two proof-of-concept movies when they complete the game - a Vulture movie and a Shocker movie. These movies represent what we thought we would be capable of creating before the project really got rolling. They also worked as a test bed for new techniques we were experimenting with at the time. I'm happy with all of the movies but if I had to pick one as my favorite it would be Mary Jane getting kidnapped.*

Q: Upon finding out that Treyarch was assigned to develop Spider-Man, what was your immediate "gut reaction" about being given the opportunity?

A: *Awesome! I've been a huge Spider-Man fan since I was a kid. I've got a pretty big comic book collection but Spider-Man was the comic I started collecting first. As a kid I studied the style of the artist who drew Spider-Man and could tell a particular artist just by looking at their drawing style. For me this is a dream come true.*

Q: What were some of the early ideas you had about the direction of the game? What sort of things didn't make it into the game?

A: *I would have liked to have more of Peter's surrounding characters like Aunt May, Harry and Mary Jane. Can you really ever have enough Mary Jane?*

Q: There are a lot of industries that require a person with your talents. What is it about the gaming industry that pulled you in and what keeps you here?

A: *I guess the most rewarding aspect of games for me is that I get the most creative control. If I worked on movies I wouldn't have nearly as much control, unless I was directing of course.*

Q: What future projects will you be working on?

A: *Well, let's just say stay tuned!*

Q: Who is your favorite Spider-Man villain in the game? Which villain would you like to have seen in the game that currently isn't?

A: *I like all of the villains in the game because each is unique in their own way. However, if I have to pick just one, it is Green Goblin because Willem's performance is wonderful and Goblin's A. I. creates the most exciting gameplay. As for who didn't make it into this one, well I know a lot of people out there would love to see Venom but I'm a big fan of some of the earlier villains like Doctor Octopus and the Lizard and I also like some of the lesser known villains like the Tarantula and Morbius.*

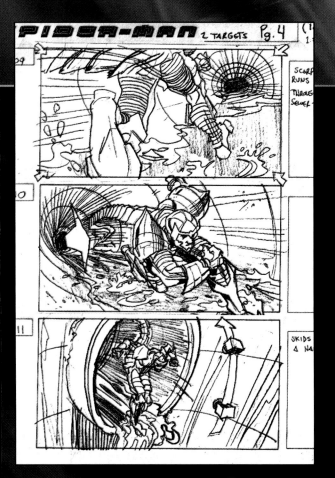

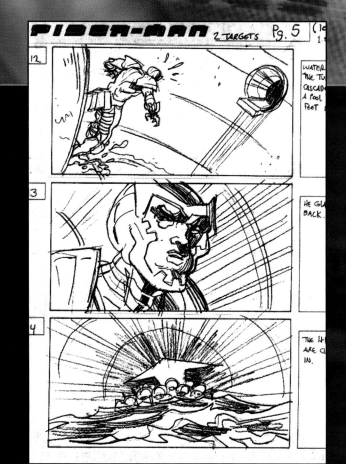

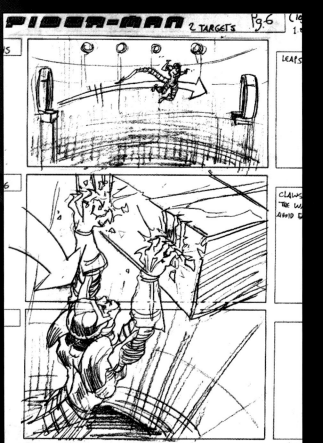

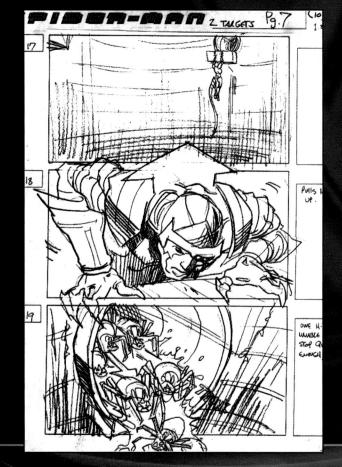

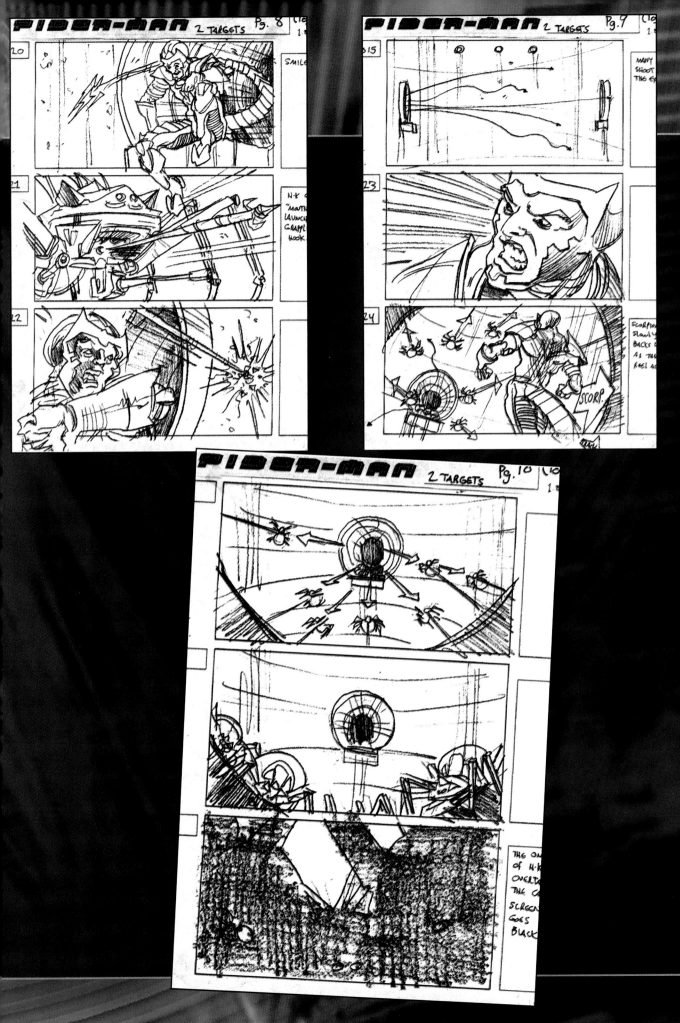

SPIDER-MAN

Level: Scorpion B   Title: Intro   Page 1 of 4

01
INT. SUBWAY PARKING STRUCTURE (ELEVATOR) - EVENING. Peter Parker, camera in hand, stands alone in the moving elevator.
Peter:
It's going to be weird going back to the subway station after my battle with Shocker.

02
Peter: (cont.)
Still, taking photos of the repairs is easy money, so I can't really complain...

03
Suddenly, the elevator lurches and stops. Peter looks up anxiously.

Level: Scorpion B   Title: Intro   Page 2 of 4

04
Peter:
"Easy money"... When will I learn to keep my mouth shut?

05A
INT. SUBWAY PARKING STRUCTURE - EVENING.
FULL Shot on elevator door.

06
Spider-Man begins prying doors open.

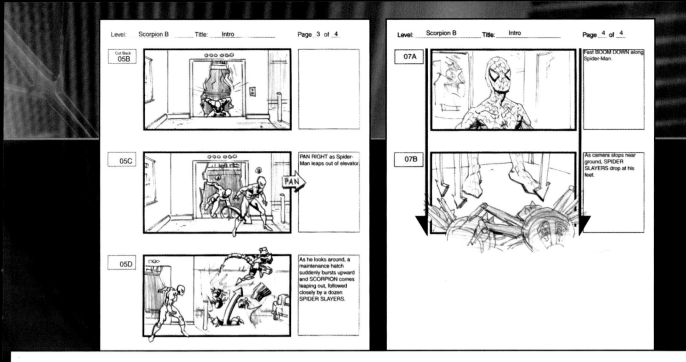

Cut Back
05B

05C

PAN RIGHT as Spider-Man leaps out of elevator.

PAN

05D

As he looks around, a maintenance hatch suddenly bursts upward and SCORPION comes leaping out, followed closely by a dozen SPIDER SLAYERS.

07A

Fast BOOM DOWN along Spider-Man.

07B

As camera stops near ground, SPIDER SLAYERS drop at his feet.

SPIDER-MAN — Level: Scorpion B — Title: Outro — Page 1 of 2
- 01A: Spider-Man opens the door leading out of the parking garage.
- 01B: SPIDER-MAN: That was tough. So what's your story, bud?
- 02: SPIDER-MAN: (cont.) Stung by a radioactive scorpion or something?

Level: Scorpion B — Title: Outro — Page 2 of 2
- 03: Keep away from me! You can't take me back there!
- 04A: Scorpion "tackles" Spider-Man. The two fly through the doorway. SPIDER-MAN: Whoa! Hey buddy! I'm just –
- 04B: The garage door slams down behind them. SCORPION: (O.C.) You're with them! I can tell! I can tell...

SPIDER-MAN — Level: Scorpion B — Title: Outro — Page 1 of 3
- 01A: Spider-Man is momentarily distracted by–
- 02: –more Spider Slayers flooding into the room, from [somewhere].
- Cut Back 01B: Scorpion takes advantage of the distraction to whack Spidey with his tail and flee. SCORPION: Aargh! Will I destroy you? Yes I will! WHACK!

Level: Scorpion B — Title: Outro — Page 2 of 3
- 03: SCORPION: Freedom! Freedom! Scorpion blasts through a grate–
- 04A: – and quickly slithers away.
- 05: SPIDER-MAN: That was just plain rude!

Level: Scorpion B — Title: Outro — Page 3 of 3
- Cut Back 04B: SPIDER-MAN: We aren't done here, Scorpion! Spider-Man quickly jumps after Scorpion.
- 04C: A trail of Spider Slayers follow.

SPIDER-MAN — Level: Scorpion C — Title: Intro — Page 1 of 2
- 01: After Spidey subdues Scorpion and the Spider-Slayers, he turns to Scorpion, lying motionless on the ground. SPIDER-MAN: I don't know who did all this to you, pal, but don't worry. We'll get you to a hospital.
- 02A: Spidey turns around and kneels to inspect one of the Spider-Slayer robots.
- 03: SPIDER-MAN: These things attacked me before...I wonder who's after me?

Level: Scorpion C — Title: Intro — Page 2 of 2
- 04: A NOISE startles Spider-Man. TILT DOWN to reveal Scorpion jumping away behind him.
- Cut Back 02B: Spider-Man turns to find that Scorpion is gone. SPIDER-MAN: Scorpion? Disappeared... I feel bad for him, but I can't help hoping I've seen the last of him...

SPIDER-MAN — Level: Scorpion C — Title: Intro — Page 1 of 1
- 01: INT. GRAND CENTRAL STATION - NIGHT Scorpion quickly runs into the subway station (now under construction from the earlier battle with Shocker). SPIDER-MAN: Let's talk about this Scorpion! You need help...
- 02A: SCORPION: Talk? No... No talking. You can't take me back!
- 02B: SPIDER-MAN: I wouldn't even know where to take you back to...

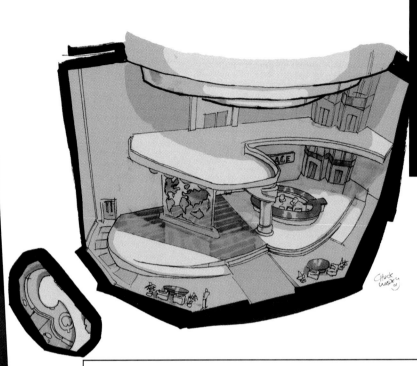

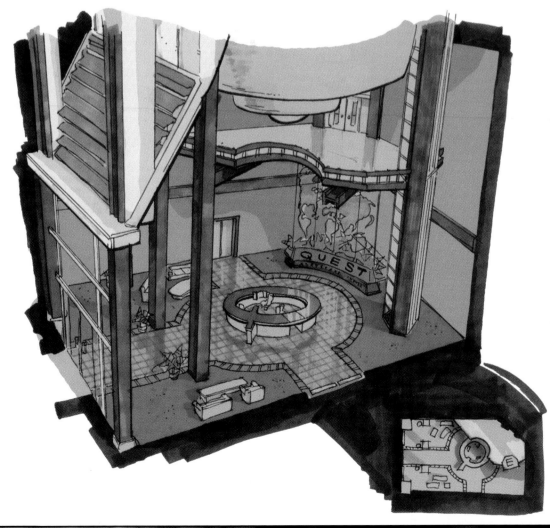

LEAD PROGRAMMER JAMES FRISTROM

HOBBIES: *Playing Videogames, Writing Fiction, Surfing*
MAJOR TITLES WORKED ON: *Die By The Sword, Tony Hawk for the Sega Dreamcast*
FAVORITE FOOD TO SNACK ON WHILE GAMING: *Beer*

FAVORITE MOVIE: *"Naked Lunch"*
MOST RECENT GAME OBSESSION: *Chrono-Trigger on Snes-9x*

Q: What was your specific role in the Spider-Man project? Or, what did your day-to-day tasks include?

A: *Everyday I would watch the schedule and the bug-list and when things broke I'd try to figure out why. I'd even pitch in and do some coding every now and then.*

Q: Upon finding out that Treyarch was assigned to develop Spider-Man, what was your immediate "gut reaction" about being given the opportunity?

A: *I thought ... can you imagine screwing that up?*

Q: What were some of the early ideas you had about the direction of the game? What sort of things didn't make it into the game?

A: *I'm not going to say but we plan to do it for the next Spider-Man and it's going to rock.*

Q: What aspect about this project in particular do you think was your favorite?

A: *The combat system and the variety it offers.*

Q: What was the trickiest task given to you and how did you solve it?

A: *Basically my job. I could write a book.*

Q: Was motion capture used on this project?

A: *No. Everyone on the team prefers hand-animation to motion capture. It's like the difference between Japanese anime and American cartoons; the Japanese hand animate and their work looks stylish, precise and cool. Americans rotoscope and it sometimes looks a little more realistic but it's just not as cool.*

Q: There are a lot of industries that require a person with your talents. What is it about the gaming industry that pulled you in and what keeps you here?

A: *It fell in my lap, really. It's all I know.*

Q: What sequence/section are you most proud of? Did a particular sequence/special move not make it into the final build? If so, why?

A: *It's a toss up between the spider-slayers and the warehouse sequence. On the one hand throwing tires at thugs is extremely satisfying, but on the other hand the way the spider-slayers move is too cool.*

In early September we had a level that was half completed that allowed players to rescue people from a burning building. But after the September 11th tragedies we removed it because we didn't want it to appear in bad taste.

Q: What future projects will you be working on?

A: *More Spider-Man, baby!*

Q: Who is your favorite Spider-Man villain in the game? Which villain would you like to have seen in the game that currently isn't?

A: *Goblin, of course. The coolest Spider-Man villain of all time is Venom but it didn't make sense to have him in this game.*

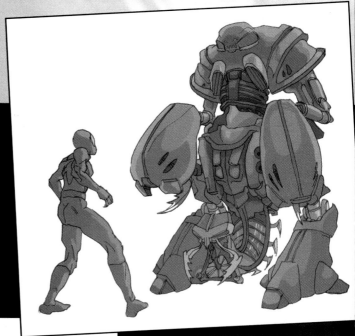

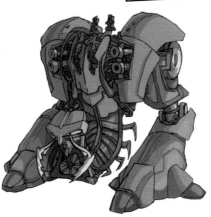

CHUCK WADEY
01

LEAD GAME DESIGNER
TOMO MORIWAKI

HOBBIES: *Games, Art, War*

MAJOR TITLES WORKED ON: *Die by the Sword, Die by the Sword: Limb from Limb, Draconus: Cult of the Wyrm, Max Steel: Covert Operations*

FAVORITE FOOD TO SNACK ON WHILE GAMING: *Cheez-its*

FAVORITE MOVIE: *"Brazil"*

MOST RECENT GAME OBSESSION: *Operation Flashpoint*

Q: What was your specific role in the Spider-Man project? Or, what did your day-to-day tasks include?

A: *Lead game designer.*

Q: Upon finding out that Treyarch was assigned to develop Spider-Man, what was your immediate "gut reaction" about being given the opportunity?

A: *I was concerned over the issues that working on a movie license could bring up.*

Q: What were some of the early ideas you had about the direction of the game? What sort of things didn't make it into the game?

A: *Several level ideas, a few characters and some plans for bosses.*

Q: What aspect about this project in particular do you think was your favorite?

A: *The team.*

Q: After completing the game, what do you expect/want people to say about the gaming experience?

A: *That it is new, challenging and memorable.*

Q: What are you most proud of concerning the game?

A: *The vast universe of options available to the player for navigating around the environments.*

Q: Who is your favorite Spider-Man villain in the game? Which villain would you like to have seen in the game that currently isn't?

A: *Goblin and Venom.*

GENERATOR

SPIDER-MAN

Level: _____ Title: _____ Page ___ of ___

SPIDER-MAN

Level: _____ Title: _____ Page ___ of ___

SPIDER-MAN

Level: _____ Title: _____ Page ___ of ___

SPIDER-MAN

Level: _____ Title: _____ Page ___ of ___

SPIDER-MAN

Level: Cityscapes B   Title: MJ safe   Page 1 of 4

01
SPIDER-MAN:
(after they reach safe spot)
Are you alright?

MARY JANE:
(still shaken)
Yeah. Thanks.

02
MARY JANE:
(a little starry-eyed)
You were great back there...

03
Spider-Man starts reluctantly backing up a little, heading back towards his waiting foe.

SPIDER-MAN:
Thanks...
(not wanting to leave)
I have to go deal with...y'know...

Level: Cityscapes B   Title: MJ safe   Page 2 of 4

CB02
MARY JANE:
Oh...yeah!
Thanks again!

CB03
SPIDER-MAN:
No problem. Grab hold of a rogue balloon anytime. Rescuing damsels is my specialty.

Spider-Man starts to web away-

04
-but MJ grabs hold of his arm and pulls him back.

Level: Cityscapes B   Title: MJ safe   Page 3 of 4

05
She gives him a quick kiss.

MARY JANE:
Go get him, Tiger!

06
View becomes full of static as if seen through an electronic device.

07
A Hunter-Killer is surveying the scene.

Level: Cityscapes B   Title: MJ safe   Page 4 of 4

08
Spider-Man web-swings away, back towards the Green Goblin.

PRODUCER JONATHAN ZAMKOFF

HOBBIES: *Sports, reading, traveling, games*

MAJOR TITLES WORKED ON: *Spider-Man for the Sega Dreamcast; this version of Spider-Man*

FAVORITE FOOD TO SNACK ON WHILE GAMING: *Honey, tangerines, candy, loads of coffee*

FAVORITE MOVIE: *"The King of New York"*

MOST RECENT GAME OBSESSION: *Samurai Showdown II (Neo Geo fighting game)*

Q: What was your specific role in the Spider-Man project? Or, what did your day-to-day tasks include?

A: *Support for the team. My job was to bulldoze away all of the clutter that got in the way of the talent. With a team of over 40 people there was so much that went into the day-to-day management that the three members of our production staff were always taxed. After reaching the QA and submission point of the project, I was responsible for directing our disc creation process to ensure our submission and QA builds were top-notch.*

Q: Although the game mimics the movie to an extent, there are some extra, classic villains that appear as bosses in the game. How did you select these characters and why?

A: *They simply made sense with our storyline and enabled us to deviate from the movie plot for game-play sake, without sacrificing plot clarity. Throwing Sandman or Doc Ock into this title, while being loads of fun, would just not have made sense.*

Q: Spider-Man is one of the most recognizable comic characters ever. What were a few of his characteristics that you definitely wanted to capture in this game? Were any limitations given concerning Spider-Man's presentation in the game?

A: *We managed to capture the strength and agility of the web slinger amazingly. We've created a huge control system that really lets the player be Spider-Man. In fact, the more one plays this game, the more they can morph themselves into every aspect of Spider-Man from his hand-to-hand combat, web slinging and smart mouthed quips. But I don't want to give too much away.*

Q: Upon finding out that Treyarch was assigned to develop Spider-Man, what was your immediate "gut reaction" about being given the opportunity?

A: *Spider-Man? Spider-Man!!! Hey I love that guy.*

Q: What were some of the early ideas you had about the direction of the game? What sort of things didn't make it into the game?

A: *We had ideas for a lot of civilian rescue and burning building motifs that we chose to remove after the tragedies of September 11th. We also had a multi-player version working that we just didn't have the time to effectively QA but I would have loved to see it in the game.*

Q: How long did this project take?

A: *Over a year and a half.*

Q: What aspect about this project in particular do you think was your favorite?

A: *This was just an awesome team to work with. From the artists, coders, scripters, sound guys, and the producers, everyone just worked their hearts out and was lots of fun to work with. We usually eat dinner together at 7:00 p.m. and the hilarious (often delirious) conversations that come out of it would definitely have won "America's Funniest Home Videos" at least 5 times.*

Q: What are you most proud of concerning this game?

A: *That after all of our hard work we have a solid AAA title that we are going to unleash on the public and cause them to stop playing all of their other games in deference.*

Q: What future projects will you be working on?

A: *Seeing the way things are going for me I'll probably be working on Spider-Man until the day I die.*

Q: Who is your favorite Spider-Man villain in the game? Which villain would you like to have seen in the game that currently isn't?

A: *My favorite villain is probably Shocker. He's your good-natured, blue-collar sort of bad guy and I'm a big fan of the average Joe super hero/super-villain. If we could have included another villain I would have probably chosen Venom. But doesn't everyone love Venom?*

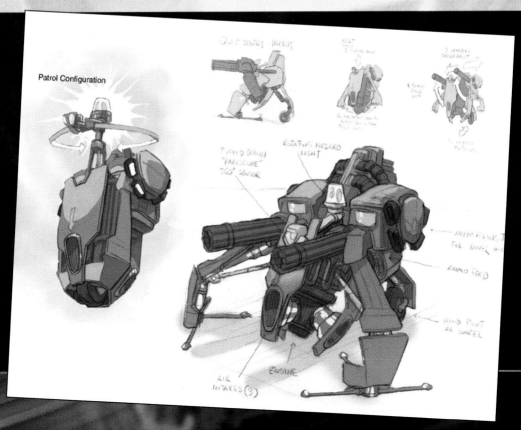

Patrol Configuration

QUEST AEROSPACE ROBOTIC SENTRY

Patrol Configuration

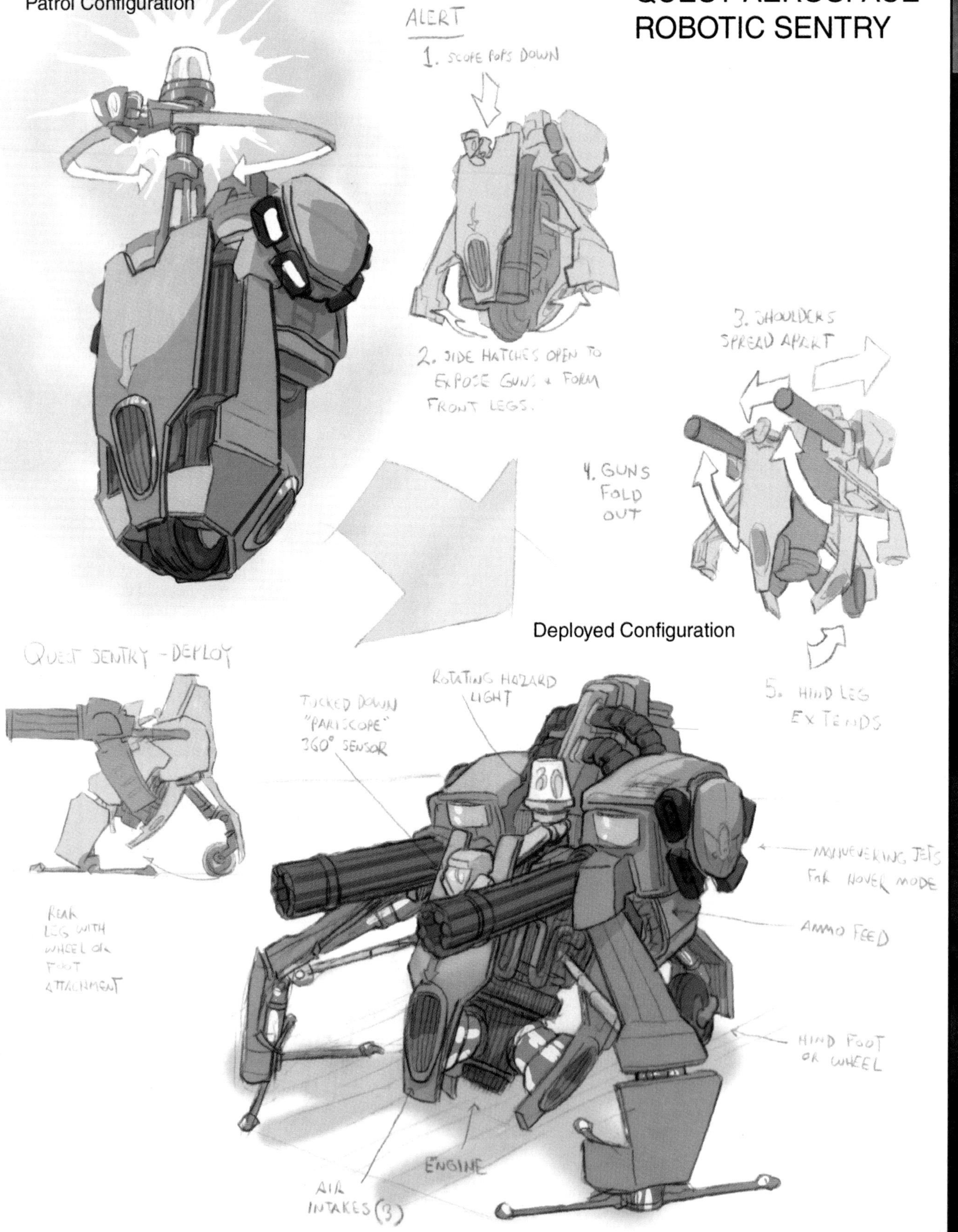
ALERT
1. SCOPE POPS DOWN
2. SIDE HATCHES OPEN TO EXPOSE GUNS & FORM FRONT LEGS.
3. SHOULDERS SPREAD APART
4. GUNS FOLD OUT
5. HIND LEG EXTENDS
QUEST SENTRY - DEPLOY
REAR LEG WITH WHEEL OR FOOT ATTACHMENT
TUCKED DOWN "PARISCOPE" 360° SENSOR
ROTATING HAZARD LIGHT
MANUEVERING JETS FOR HOVER MODE
AMMO FEED
HIND FOOT OR WHEEL
ENGINE
AIR INTAKES (3)

Deployed Configuration

01

EXT. NEW YORK CITY (DOWNTOWN) - NIGHT

Spidey rushes to disarm the bombs before they explode.

SPIDER-MAN: I've got to disarm those devices!

02

EXT. ROOFTOP ABOVE NEW YORK - NIGHT
Light mechs, left by Green Goblin, assemble electromagnetic pulse emitters.

03

A Mech drops off the base of one E.M.P. emitter.

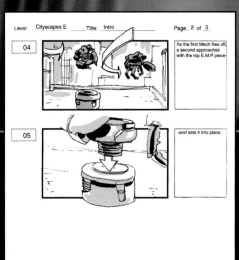

04

As the first Mech flies off, a second approaches with the top E.M.P. piece-

05

-and sets it into place.

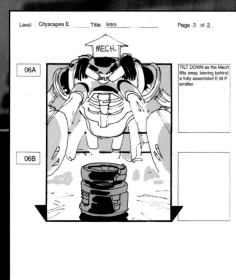

06A

MECH.

TILT DOWN as the Mech lifts away, leaving behind a fully assembled E.M.P. emitter.

06B

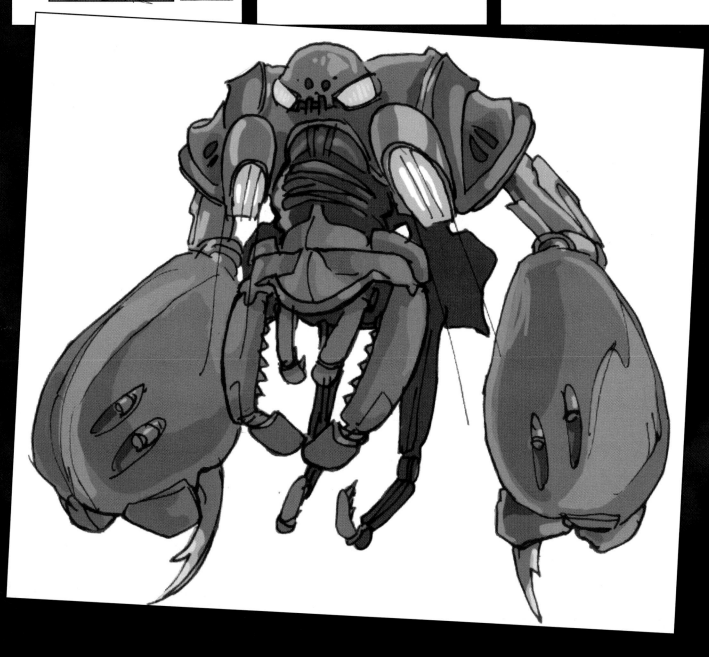

AUDIO DIRECTOR SERGIO A. BUSTAMANTE II

HOBBIES: Soccer

MAJOR TITLES WORKED ON: *Space Invaders (1999), Draconus: Cult of the Wyrm, Max Steel: Covert Missions, Tony Hawk's Pro Skater 2X and NHL 2K2.*

FAVORITE FOOD TO SNACK ON WHILE GAMING: Coffee

FAVORITE MOVIE: *"The Right Stuff"*

MOST RECENT GAME OBSESSION: *Spider-Man*

Q: What was your specific role in the Spider-Man project? Or, what did your day-to-day tasks include?

A: *I was the audio director for the game and I managed a team of three sound designers and audio sub contractors. It was my task to be the glue that kept the audio team together and focused on creating the best sound possible for the game. I also supervised the music and VO for the game.*

Q: What "mood" did you want to set with the music? What sort of inspiration do you use (personal music favorites, etc.)?

A: *I wanted a very "cinematic" mood to the music in the game. We knew we had this awesome movie license and I wanted to make sure we remained true to the themes and quality that the film has. I also wanted to make sure we had an "edge" so that is why we hired composer Michael McCuistion. Michael was fresh off winning an Emmy Award for "Batman Beyond" and I really like his style and ability to merge orchestral tracks with the latest electronic/synth tracks. We recorded all of the orchestral parts using a live orchestra in Prague, Czech Republic. The blend of those tracks and the synth tracks work really well in the game.*

Q: Were you given total control over the project, or were you provided with a specific direction? Where do you start? Do you wait to see the game...?

A: *"Total control" sounds a bit much so let's just say I had a "major influence" on how all of the sound in the game was incorporated and in which direction the sound should take. I always welcome input and was fortunate to have the input of our creative director and senior producer. They were a tremendous help throughout the project and were always on hand when I had music or sound design ideas to present.*

I started at the beginning with everyone else on the project. That's what's great about being part of the staff. I get to watch the game develop from its conception and throw in my 2 cents (ok, more like 20 cents) in regard to sound as the game progresses.

Q: There are a lot of industries that require a person with your talents. What is it about the gaming industry that pulled you in and what keeps you here?

A: *I love how the industry is always changing and how we all have to keep up with it. I'm fortunate that my aspect in the industry requires a bit of creativity and not just technical know how. The two really have a symbiotic relationship, but the creativity keeps it fun.*

Q: What is your favorite piece in the game?

A: *Well, in regard to the music, they're all wonderful and well-composed pieces however the one that stands out for me is the Green Goblin piece. It really captures the tortured villain that the Green Goblin is. Another piece, if you get to it, is the "bowling" piece. It's a gem.*

Q: What is your favorite type of music?

A: *I listen to everything so I don't really have a "favorite" but if you were to look at my CD collection you would find a lot of techno, trance, R&B, house and good ol' rock n' roll. Uh, and don't tell, but I also have a bit of classical and opera in there as well.*

Q: What's your favorite part about working on a game?

A: *I enjoy the entire collaborative process of working on a game. I'm just one piece of a grand puzzle that makes everything work. I'm fortunate enough to have an opportunity to work with all of the talented artists, animators, programmers, designers, voiceover actors and almost everyone related to the project.*

Q: What future projects will you be working on?

A: *Chances are if it has a Treyarch logo on it I'm involved on the sound side.*

Q: Who is your favorite Spider-Man villain in the game? Which villain would you like to have seen in the game that currently isn't?

A: *The Green Goblin! Working with Willem Dafoe for the VO was a great experience and I really feel he captured something special for our game. He truly was a "villain" but the character also has a lot of depth and personality. Willem was excellent in capturing all of this in his acting and really leant his voice talents to us on a grand scale.*

Black Cat. Is she a villain? Ah, I don't care … I would have liked to see her in our game.

KRAVEN™

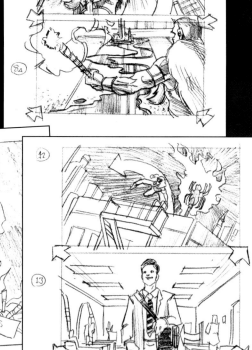

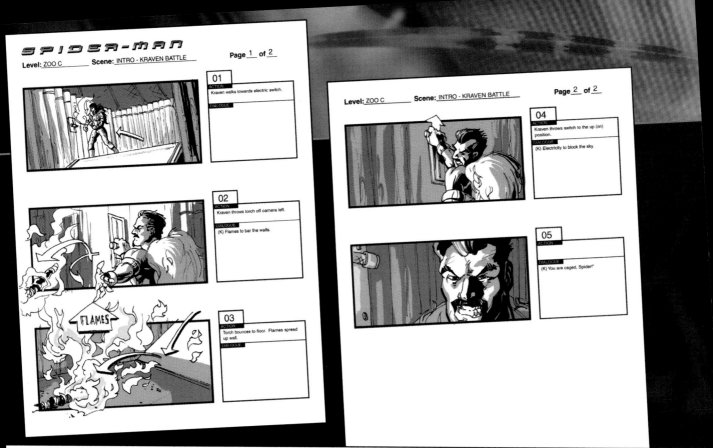

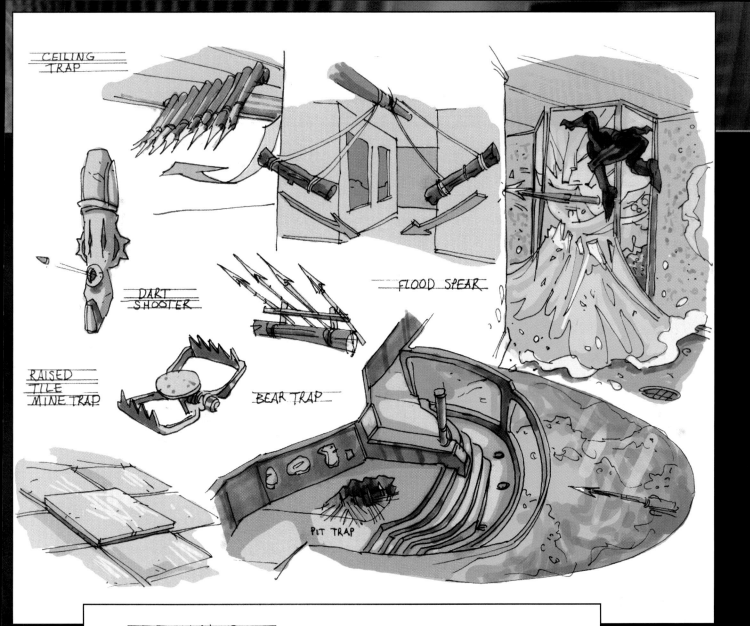

CEILING
TRAP

DART
SHOOTER

FLOOD SPEAR

RAISED
TILE
MINE TRAP

BEAR TRAP

PIT TRAP

VETERINARY LAB
OFFICES - ANIMAL KITCHEN

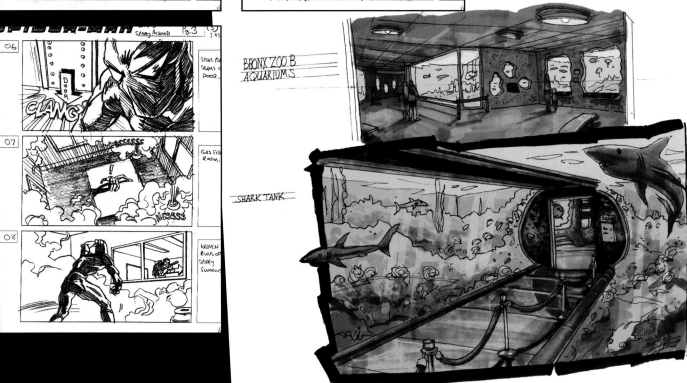

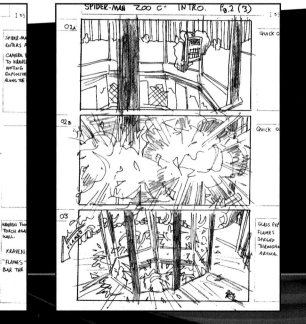

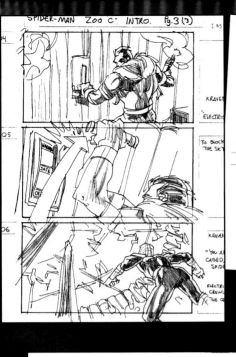

BIG SHOW
ROOM

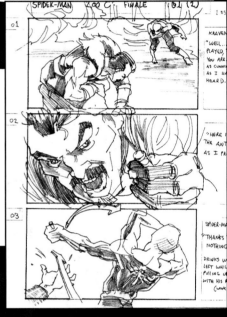

VARIOUS
WALL TANKS

SNAKE SHOW ENTRANCE

LAZER
SECURITY
SYSTEM

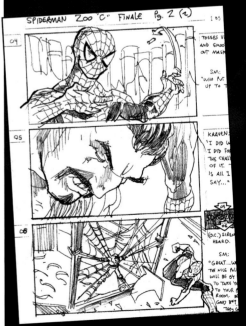

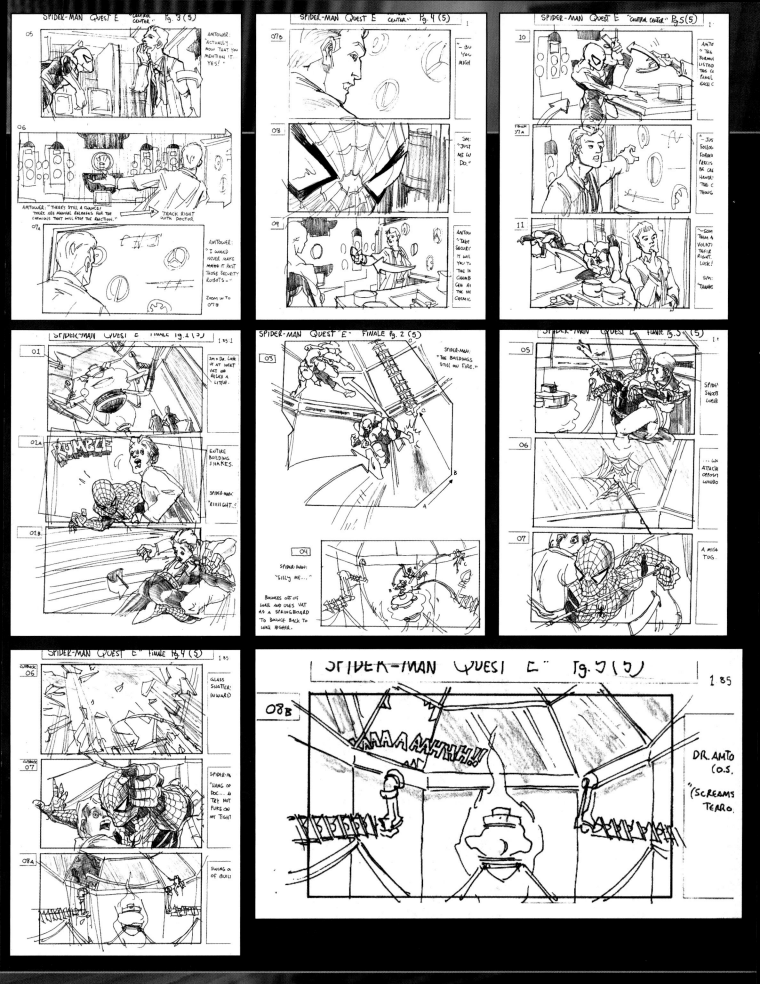

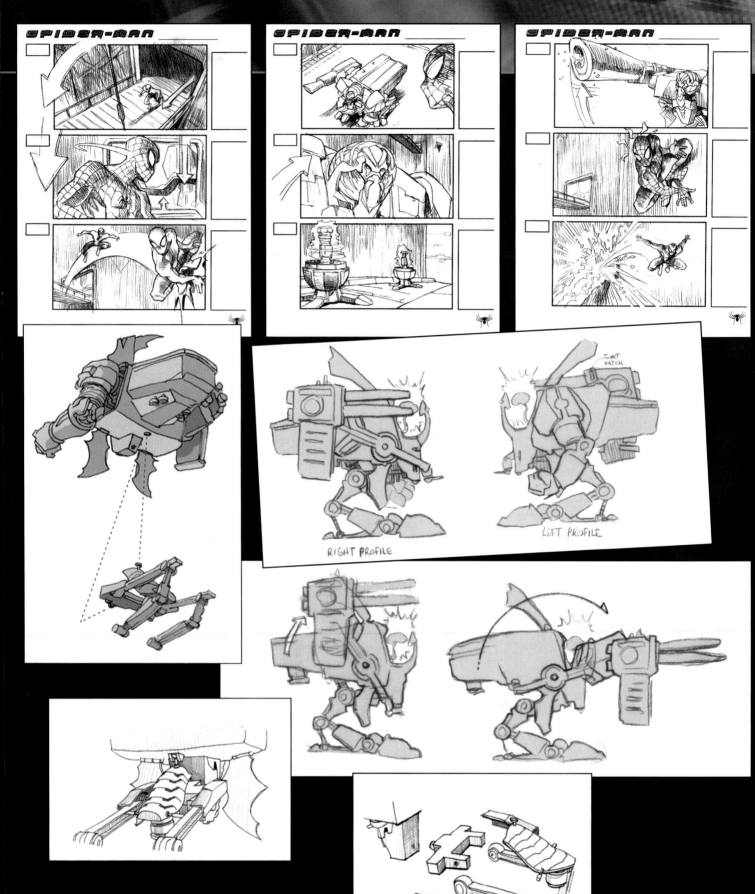

CHIEF ENGINEER JASON BARE

HOBBIES: *Gaming and programming*

MAJOR TITLES WORKED ON: *Draconus, Max Steel*

FAVORITE FOOD TO SNACK ON WHILE GAMING: *Pizza & Mountain Dew*

FAVORITE MOVIE: *"Lord of the Rings"*

MOST RECENT GAME OBSESSION: *Medal of Honor: Allied Assault*

Q: What was your specific role in the Spider-Man project? Or, what did your day-to-day tasks include?

A: *I was the Chief Engineer on the project and my team and I were responsible for updating and maintaining the ArchEngine and making sure the game designers were fully supported. I co-designed and wrote the AI system along with several individual AI's in the game. I also designed and wrote the Spider-Man player controls.*

Q: Upon finding out that Treyarch was assigned to develop Spider-Man, what was your immediate "gut reaction" about being given the opportunity?

A: *Simply put, I was excited about the project and thought that this was a title that would indeed be a great challenge. There are not many super heroes as technically demanding in a game like Spider-Man and how often do you get a hero that can crawl on walls, swing though the air with the greatest of ease and basically go anywhere he wants to?*

Q: What were some of the early ideas you had about the direction of the game? What sort of things didn't make it into the game?

A: *I wanted to streamline Spider-Man's control scheme and make it easier to execute web-attacks and perform special moves. My goal was to make the controls easy for new players (or players of previous Spider-Man games) to grasp and to allow for more advanced controls as the player gains experience playing the game.*

Indeed, a few things did not get into the game. We had to let go of a few ideas about using web yanking in creative ways due to time pressures and a few of the AI designs also fell onto the cutting room floor during the course of the project.

Q: What aspect about this project in particular do you think was your favorite?

A: *Working on the AI system was my favorite. We wrote it from scratch, so it was fascinating to see the characters begin to react to their environment. Sometimes we were surprised by how smart they would behave and how cool they looked just moving around (like the Spider Slayers and the Green Goblin on his glider). It was also a challenge to make characters that could deal with Spider-Man's unique movement abilities.*

Q: After completing the game, what do you expect/want people to say about the gaming experience?

A: *I would like people to say they had fun playing the game and that they want to play it again! We've put a lot of secrets and bonuses into the game for good replay value.*

Q: What are you most proud of concerning the game?

A: *It would have to be the control scheme and the combat system because it is very open ended. Beginning players can easily grasp the basics and just have fun with the game. As players become more advanced, the system opens up to reveal nearly infinite means of dispatching your foes. Every way that Spider-Man moves - swinging, jumping, standing, zipping, etc. - can be turned into an attack with just a few button presses. Many different types of attacks can be chained together instead of having just standard punch and kick combos.*

Q: Spider-Man's extreme flexibility adds a special characteristic to him that other heroes don't have. Which of his in-game moves was most difficult to create?

A: *This is a good question and Jim, [James Zachary, lead animator] should probably answer it. One problem that occurs when working with a character as flexible and agile as Spider-Man is being able to create moves that are both heroic and dynamic, without going overboard. The moves, no matter how off the wall they are, must be believable and fun, you want the player to get excited over the animations and to feel a little adrenaline pulse through the controller. You never want the player to realize, or even think for a second, that Spider-Man's moves are not real, or that, in reality, they are physically impossible. Thoughts like that pull people out of the game. It happens all the time in movies - the hero/heroine is stuck in a tight spot, enemies are closing in, he/she jumps on a sports car (which happens to have the keys in it), pops a wheelie, knocks over the guy with the missile launcher, jams on the front break, flip over some dudes, grabs hold of an un-expecting passing pigeon which gives them enough momentum to plow through the on coming army with out messing up their hair. You laugh at the ridiculousness of it and check your watch wondering when the madness will end.*

There is a fine line that we walk in creating fantasy and we need to push the envelope right up to the edge of that believability cliff, but we don't want to fall off. In Spider-Man, that cliff was difficult to climb in dealing with the combo moves. We tried to make them fun, dynamic, entertaining and, for the most part, somewhat believable within the Spider-Man universe. Still, there were plenty of moves tossed into the recycle bin because they were just a bit too far out there. Even Spider-Man, with all of the flipping, jumping and twisting, has his limits. Good news for Spider-Man contortion fans - every year the envelope of reality gets pushed a bit further so who knows, maybe you will see some of those moves splashing around in our next game.

Q: Which of Spider-Man's animations were the most difficult to program? The least difficult?

A: *His crawling was the most difficult to program. We wanted to create more realistic, and thus more complicated, environments for Spider-Man to explore. Allowing for him to crawl on as many surfaces as possible became quite difficult as the geometry increased in complexity.*

The least difficult was the "Yo-Yo" move. Chris Soares walked into my office one morning saying that it would be cool if Spider-Man could hang upside down from a web like in the comics. A couple of hours later I had it up and running as a simple modification to the zipping controls.

Q: What future projects will you be working on?

A: *Hopefully another Spider-Man game!*

Q: Who is your favorite Spider-Man villain in the game? Which villain would you like to have seen in the game that currently isn't?

A: *That's a tough question ... I like a lot of the villains we have because each is unique in their own way. Since I have to choose, I guess I'd say the Green Goblin. He is a lot of fun to fight when he's flying around on his glider and he is a very challenging foe when he is on the ground.*

One villain I would have liked to see would have been Venom. It would have given us another chance to have an enemy with some of the same movement abilities as Spider-Man.

Oscorp SuperMech

Final battle platform - Spider man destroys the brain.

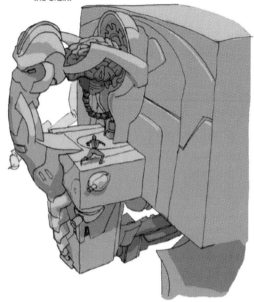

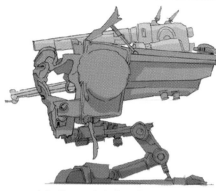

Left profile - arm omitted to illustrate leg

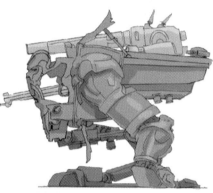

Left profile - with gorilla arm

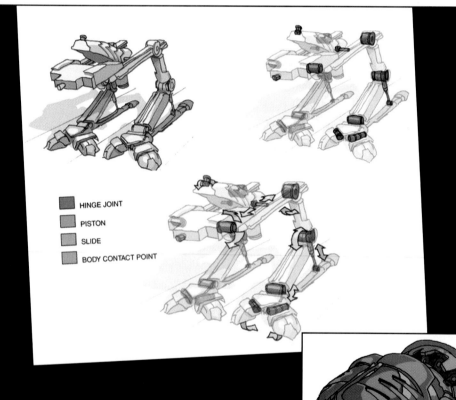

■ HINGE JOINT

□ PISTON

□ SLIDE

□ BODY CONTACT POINT

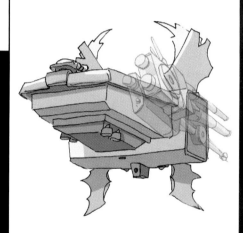

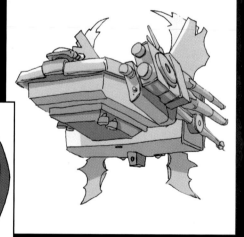

Oscorp SuperMech

Spider man's course of battle...
1. Scale the Mech's massive surface while, 2., avoiding gun fire. 3. He finds his way to a control hatch on the mech's giant turret, where he takes command and uses the weapon to destroy the generator powering the mech brain's protective force field. 4. Returning to the lower platform, Spidey finds that the brain is now vulnerable to his attack.

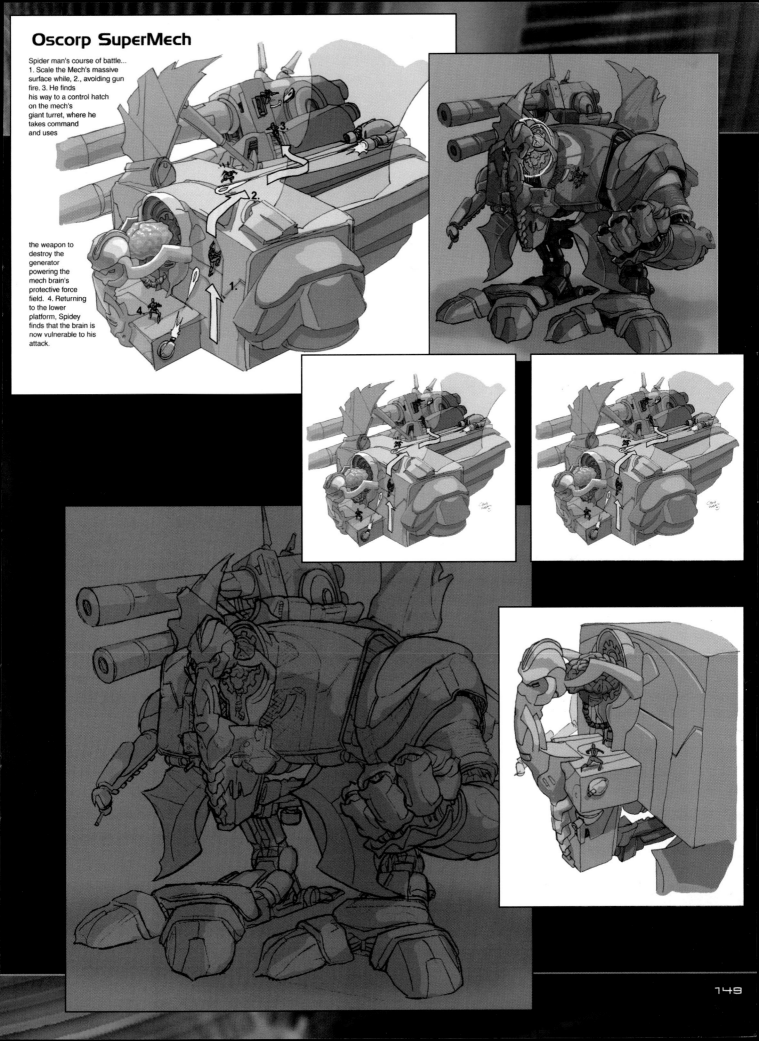

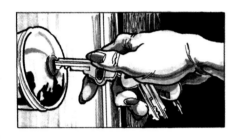

FINALE

SPIDER-MAN

Level: Bridge A   Title: Intro

01

EXT. NEAR MARY JANE'S APARTMENT - NIGHT

Spider-Man, web-swinging as fast as he can, closes in on Mary Jane's apartment.

02

As he gets closer, he sees the smoke trail of Green Goblin's glider.

03

SPIDER-MAN

Too late! -

Level: Bridge A   Title: Intro

04

-Don't worry, Mary Jane. I'm coming.

Spidey banks to alter course and follow the Goblin's trail. In the distance, Goblin's LAUGHTER continues to echo through the city.

SPIDER-MAN

Level: Bridge A   Title: Outro

01

GREEN GOBLIN

We're almost there, hero. Let's finally settle our feud.

02

SPIDER-MAN

Just put Mary Jane down safely and then we'll see how tough you really are!

SPIDER-MAN

Level: Bridge C   Title: Intro

01

02

Green Goblin places Mary Jane at the top of a bridge platform.

03

Mary Jane collapses to her knees.

Level: Bridge C   Title: Intro

04

Goblin flies away from her; he extends his hand-

05

-and waves Spider-Man towards him.

Green Goblin

C'mon, punk. Let's do this...

SPIDER-MAN

Level: Bridge C   Title: Outro

01

EXT. QUEENSBOROUGH BRIDGE - NIGHT

Defeated by Spider-Man, Green Goblin struggles to his feet. He pulls off his mask, revealing himself to be-

02

-Norman Osborn. Spider-Man is stunned. How could this man, the father of his best friend, be such a murderous enemy?

03

SPIDER-MAN:
[SMEND001.WAV]
(hurt and stunned)
Mr. Osborn... Why...?

Level: Bridge C   Title: Outro

04

As Spider-Man stares at Norman in dismay, the Goblin Glider is moving into position directly behind him.

NORMAN OSBORN:
[NOEND001.WAV]
(panting)
Surprised? Yes...

05 Goblin Glider P.O.V.

NORMAN OSBORN:
(Cont'd)
I suppose you would be...

06

NORMAN OSBORN:
(Cont'd)
but the best surprise...is still to come...

Level: Bridge C   Title: Outro

07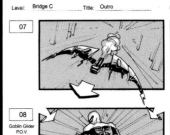

The Glider shoots forward-

08 Goblin Glider P.O.V. FAST TRUCK IN

-but Spider-Man's Spider Sense warns him at the last moment.

Level: Bridge C   Title: Outro

09B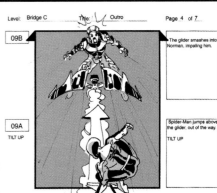

The glider smashes into Norman, impaling him.

09A TILT UP

Spider-Man jumps above the glider, out of the way.

TILT UP

09C

FADE

EXCITING EXTRAS

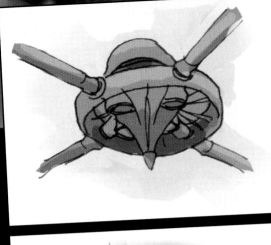

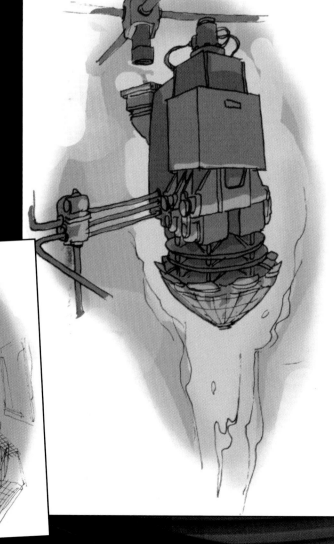

SENIOR PRODUCER GREGORY JOHN

Q: We know that there are a lot of stages and elements that go into the development of a game. (Storyboards, concept art, sound and music production, programming, voice, etc.) Could you explain the process and order in which these occur?

A: *We began with a rough outline of the movie and then built around that with more villains and gameplay that would tie-in well with the movie's plot. Additionally, we concentrated on creating new modes of gameplay by trying to come up with stuff that videogame players had never before experienced. For example, aerial combat was born out of that together with having a villain that can fly (Green Goblin).*

Q: With this game being so closely tied to a movie, did you already have a lot of the resources supplied to you that would normally have had to be created in-house?

A: *The look and feel of our game, as well as the plot, is heavily influenced by the movie but even with all of the resources from the film, we had to adapt it specifically for a video game. Because our team has worked on a previous Spider-Man game we had a good idea of what needed to be done.*

Q: With so many different aspects of a game being worked on simultaneously, what priorities have to be set in order to maintain a timely schedule? Is there a specific process that would cause everything else to stop if it wasn't on schedule?

A: *Gameplay was our number one priority. We would sacrifice other aspects of our schedule to make sure gameplay concerns were addressed.*

Q: Are there ever issues with having developed "perfect" elements of a game that simply can't be integrated? For example, would the situation occur where you have incredible music and a fantastic cinematic sequence that simply don't work well together?

A: *This is where keeping priorities straight is very important and we always need to remind ourselves that gameplay elements come first, then code issues need to be addressed. Also, the art for videogames has a very technical aspect to it so any art issues such as memory constraints, etc. also need to be addressed. With the music and cinematic sequences it is a question of efficiency, that is, of how much work would be required to make them work well together.*

Q: With the leaps in technology, especially with the next generation platforms, do you find that you need to take on more responsibilities? Have you begun to expand the types of operations that occur within Treyarch? Have you had to hire people for positions that simply didn't exist two years ago?

A: *This biggest impact of the popularity of the next generation platforms is that we have to do simultaneous, cross-platform development. This hasn't created new positions but it does mean the teams need to be larger in order to handle the code and data for all of the platforms.*

Q: As a development company, what are the most exciting operations concerning game creation that occur under your roof?

A: *I think the most excitement is generated when someone does something new and never before seen. When a programmer comes up with an Artificial Intelligence system for an enemy and we get to see Spider-Man fighting against it, it's very cool. When an artist paints an ultra-realistic sky and we see it for the first time, it really can take your breath away.*

Q: This game is being simultaneously released on three consoles. What were some of the issues that arose concerning this situation? Are there any programming complications that occurred that needed to be circumvented? Or was it a relatively easy process?

A: *A greater degree of resources and organization was required for simultaneous, cross-platform development but I don't think we ran into complications that we wouldn't have run into on each console by itself. It is not an easy process though and decisions have to be made very carefully to accommodate all three platforms.*

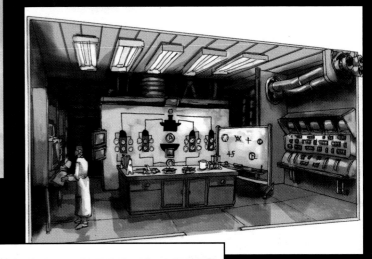

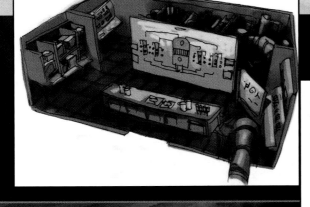

ELEVATOR
SHAFT

MECH
HOLES

CONTROL
ROOM

MIRROR

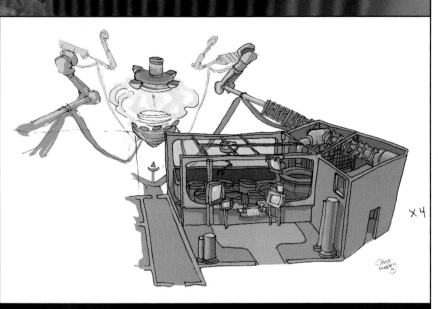

×4

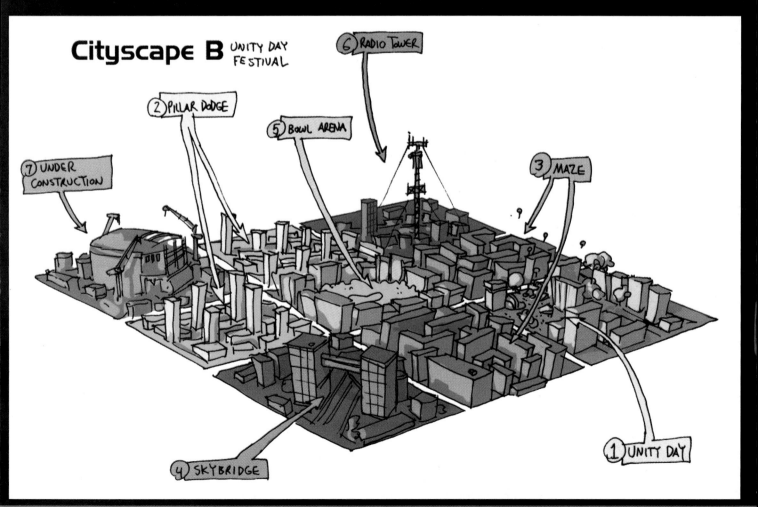

Cityscape B UNITY DAY FESTIVAL

6 RADIO TOWER

2 PILLAR DODGE

5 BOWL ARENA

7 UNDER CONSTRUCTION

3 MAZE

4 SKYBRIDGE

1 UNITY DAY

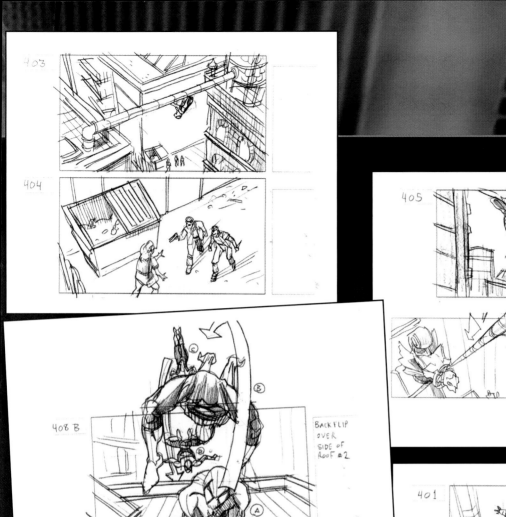

403

404

405

ROOF2
ROOF1

408 B

BACKFLIP
OVER
SIDE OF
ROOF #2

409

DESCENDS ON
MUGGERS.

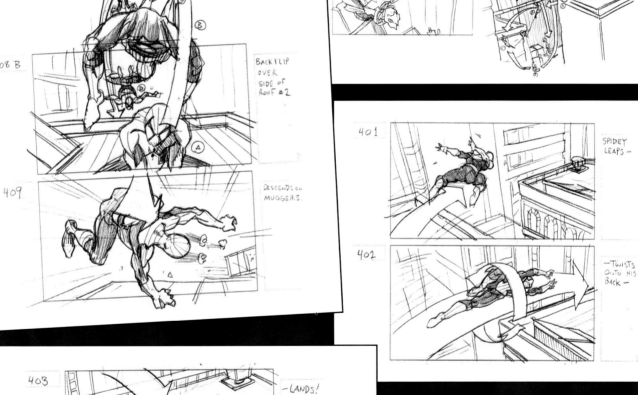

401

SPIDEY
LEAPS —

402

— TWISTS
ONTO HIS
BACK —

403

— LANDS!

403 B

CAMERA PULLS
BACK TO
SHOW THAT
SM IS VIDEO
FOOTAGE
PLAYING ON A
MONITOR IN
OBSCURE
LOCATION
LABS

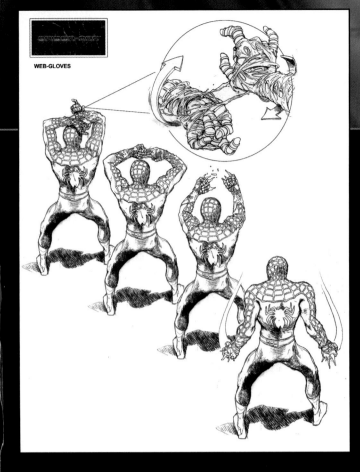

WEB-GLOVES

WEB-DOME

WEB BALL ATTACK

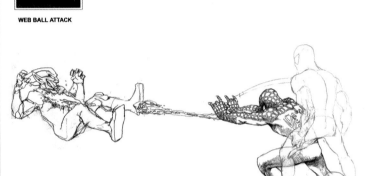

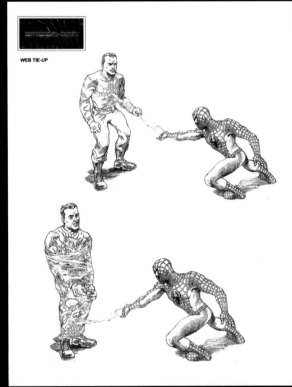

WEB TIE-UP

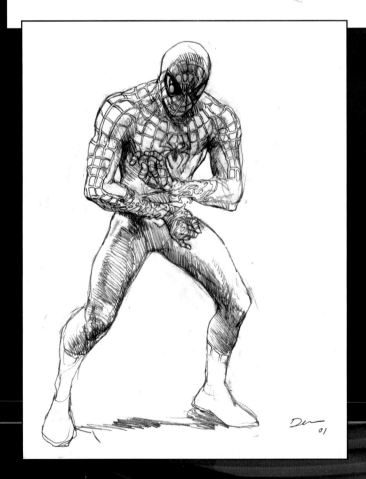

SECRETS

UNLOCKING SCHEDULE

Here's what you get if you beat the game on the various levels.

Play the game to unlock certain Sony Production Art and game production extras. You can take a look at these in the Movie Viewer.

Beat the game to open some secrets. Depending on which Difficulty you play on, you'll gain access to different secrets.

DIFFICULTY	UNLOCK
Easy	Extra Skin: Wrestling Costume
Normal	Extra Skin: Alex Ross Green Goblin
Hero/Superhero	Playable Movie: Green Goblin

Once you've beaten the game, a Secret Store will open in the Special Menu. Here are the prices of what's available for purchase.

POINTS	PURCHASE
10,000	Pinhead Bowling
20,000	Vulture Movie
30,000	Shocker Animation Test
50,000	Unlimited Webbing

OBJECTIVE REQUIREMENTS

Certain objectives require you to beat the clock or kill enough villains. This list will tell you what you need to do on the various difficulties to complete the objectives.

LEVEL	OBJECTIVE REQUIREMENTS
Search for Revenge	Kill 15 Thugs
Warehouse Hunt	Stealth - Avoid detection by the thugs in the first chopshop room until you see the boss thug movie.
Birth of a Hero	Easy Time - 900 seconds Normal Time - 500 seconds Hero/Superhero Time - 300 seconds
OsCorp's Gambit	Destroy 5 Hunter Killer Robots (Hero Superhero only)
The Subway Station	Time - 120 seconds
Chase Through the Sewers	Easy Time - 800 seconds Easy Thugs - Kill 30 Thugs Normal Time - 600 seconds Normal Thugs - Kill 40 Thugs Hero/Superhero Time - 400 seconds Hero/Superhero Thugs - Kill 40 Thugs
Showdown with Shocker	Easy Time - 500 seconds Normal Time - 250 seconds Hero/Superhero Time - 120 seconds
Vulture's Lair	Time - 240 seconds
Vulture Escapes	Time - 300 seconds Proximity - Stay within 30m of the Vulture for 4 seconds
Air Duel with Vulture	Time - 120 seconds
Corralled	Scorpion Health - Complete level with Scorpion having over 50% health

LEVEL	OBJECTIVE REQUIREMENTS
Scorpion's Rampage	No Pick-ups - Don't pick up any Health or Web Cartridges
Chemical Chaos	Stealth - Don't activate the alarm Time - 400 seconds
Coup d-Etat	Easy Time - 480 seconds Normal Time - 350 seconds Hero/Superhero Time - 270 seconds
The Offering	Time - 400 seconds Ride Goblin - Jump on his Glider 3 or more times
Race Against Time	Easy Time - 300 seconds Normal Time - 210 seconds Hero/Superhero Time - 170 seconds
The Razor's Edge	Destroy 75 Razorbats Easy - Fewer than 2 Pick-ups and over 75 Health Normal - Fewer than 3 Pick-ups and over 100 Health Hero/Superhero - Fewer than 5 Pick-ups and over 150 Health
Breaking and Entering	Stealth - Never Activate the Alarm Easy Time - 480 seconds Normal Time - 360 seconds Hero/Superhero Time - 240 seconds
Escape from OsCorp	Destroy 10 or more Super Soldiers
OsCorp's Ultimate Weapon	Time - 400 seconds

MY SPIDER-SENSE IS TINGLING!

Lastly, you may have been playing long enough to notice that your spider-sense is tingling when you look at the poster included in this guide. What could it be?

SPIDER-MAN®
OFFICIAL STRATEGY GUIDE

by Phillip Marcus

Brady Publishing

An Imprint of Pearson Education
201 West 103rd Street
Indianapolis, Indiana 46290

ISBN: 0-7440-0160-9

Library of Congress Catalog No.: 2002104292

Printing Code: The rightmost double-digit number is the year of the book's printing; the rightmost single-digit number is the number of the book's printing. For example, 01-1 shows that the first printing of the book occurred in 2001.

05 04 03 02   4 3 2 1

Manufactured in the United States of America.

BRADYGAMES STAFF

Publisher	**David Waybright**
Editor-In-Chief	**H. Leigh Davis**
Creative Director	**Robin Lasek**
Marketing Manager	**Janet Eshenour**
Assistant Licensing Manager	**Mike Degler**
Assistant Marketing Manager	**Susie Nieman**

CREDITS

Title Manager	**Tim Cox**
Project Editor	**Christian Sumner**
Screenshot Editor	**Michael Owen**
Book Designers	**Kurt Owens**
	Carol Stamile
Production Designer	**Tracy Wehmeyer**

ACTIVISION STRATEGY GUIDE CREDITS

Strategy Guide Co-Producers	**Justin Berenbaum** **Brian Pass**	Additional Conceptual Art	**Ian Diesen Hosfeld**
Conceptual Art and Storyboards	**Chuck Wadey**	User Interface	**Andrew Swihart**
		High Resolution Green Goblin Model	**Blur Studios**

TREYARCH ART TEAM

Art Direction	**Chris Soares**		**Brian Morrisroe**
3D Characters	**Arnold Agraviador**		**Jake Santa Ana**
	Brad Grace		**Wendy Davis**
	Kevin Pasko	Environments	**Travis Eastepp**
	Michael McMahn		**Brian Morrisroe**
High Resolution Head Models	**Tim Smilovitch**		**Jake Santa Ana**
	Jon Lauf		**Tony Kwok**
	Dusty Peterson		**Ian Diesen Hosfeld**
	Michael McMahn		**Wendy Davis**
Rendered Character Images	**Ryan Duffin**		**Michael McMahn**
	Ian Diesen Hosfeld		**Peter Chen**
			Chris Erdman
Lead Level Builder	**Alex Bortoluzzi**		
Map Images	**Travis Eastepp**		

BRADYGAMES ACKNOWLEDGEMENTS

BradyGames would like to thank the following people for their help on this guide.

From Activision: John Heineke, Matt Geyer, Lisa Fields, Michael Hand, Matt Powers, Jason Potter, Henry Peter Villanueva, Kragen Lum, Marilena Rixford, Joe Favazza, and Sam Nouriani.

From Sony Pictures Consumer Products: Mark Caplan, Eric Thomsen, Laetitia May, and Paige Brown.

MARVEL®
www.marvel.com